Betty Crocker's

COMPLETE CHICKEN COOKBOOK

Betty Crocker's

COMPLETE CHICKEN COOKBOOK

MACMILLAN • USA

MACMILLAN
A Prentice Hall Macmillan Company
15 Columbus Circle
New York, New York 10023

Library of Congress Cataloging-in-Publication Data

Crocker, Betty.
[complete chicken cookbook]
Betty Crocker's complete chicken cookbook.
p.   cm.
Includes index.
ISBN 0-671-89243-6
1. Cookery (Chicken)   I. Title.   II. Title: Complete chicken
cookbook.
TX750.5.C45C77   1994
641.6′65—dc20   93-44974
                                                 CIP

Designed by Irving Perkins Associates, Inc.

Manufactured in the United States of America

10   9   8   7   6   5   4   3   2   1

First Edition

Front cover: Fiesta Chicken Breasts (page 93)
Back cover: Chicken-Barley Stew with Cheddar Dumplings (page 126)

Contents

Introduction

Everyone seems to love chicken, from classic roast chicken with stuffing, to fresh new ideas including pizzas and appetizers. But, no one ever seems to have enough chicken recipes to satisfy their cravings for poultry.

That's why we created *Betty Crocker's Complete Chicken Cookbook*, to bring you more than 175 recipes for delicious chicken and turkey dishes. From homey Chicken with Potato Stuffing and Chicken Tetrazzini to the tantalizing flavors of Tequila Chicken with Fettuccine, Jamaican Jerk Chicken and Peanut Butter–Chile Chicken, you're sure to love the wide variety of recipes here.

First, whole roast chicken is showcased, along with recipes for roast turkey and Rock Cornish Hens. Roast Turkey with Cherry-Rye Stuffing or Southwest Roast Chicken will add excitement to your repertoire. Next you'll find great ideas for chicken pieces and parts, including Crunchy Hazelnut Chicken and Sun-dried Tomato and Apricot Chicken.

Chicken and turkey breasts are incredibly versatile, and the recipes here make that abundantly clear. You'll love Black and White Chili, Curried Chicken Kabobs and Chicken Quesadilla Sandwiches. And we all want drumsticks! Try Cashew Drumsticks or Turkey Drumsticks with Spicy Barbecue Sauce. When it comes to wings, you'll find both appetizers and main-dish selections. Buffalo Chicken Wings are a sure-fire party hit, and Chinese Chicken Wings a spicy main-dish treat.

You'll find wonderful recipes for convenient cuts of chicken, as well as a chapter of "expressly" easy recipes using precooked deli poultry or savory leftovers. And, we added a chapter on condiments to spark your chicken dishes, from Honey-Mustard Spread, to Tropical Fruit Salsa. Finally there is a wonderfully handy Poultry Primer, to help you buy, store and handle chicken safely.

Betty Crocker's Complete Chicken Cookbook is not only chock-full of great chicken recipes, it also answers all your poultry questions, from roasting times, to seasoning savvy. We think you'll find this is the chicken cookbook that is indispensable!

The Betty Crocker Editors

Poultry Primer

TYPES OF CHICKEN

Buying chicken can be confusing when you see the variety in your local market. The information below describes the most commonly available types of chicken and will help you to buy just what you want.

- **Broiler-fryer:** This all-purpose chicken weighs from 3 to 3½ pounds, and your best bargain is buying the whole bird. Larger birds will have a higher ratio of meat to bone. Allow about ¾ pound (bone-in) per serving. Cut-up chicken and boneless chicken parts, such as breasts and thighs, will cost more per pound, but do offer greater convenience.

- **Roaster:** This chicken is a little older and larger than the broiler-fryer, weighing 4 to 6 pounds, and has tender meat that is ideal for roasting.

- **Stewing:** This chicken (also referred to as hen) weighs 4½ to 6 pounds and provides a generous amount of meat. It is a mature, less tender bird and is best cooked by simmering or in stews and soups.

- **Rock Cornish Hen:** These small young, specially bred chickens (also referred to as game hens) weigh 1 to 1½ pounds and have all white meat. Allow one-half to one hen per person. Most supermarkets carry hens in the freezer case.

WHAT SHOULD I LOOK FOR WHEN BUYING CHICKEN OR TURKEY?

Selecting fresh, wholesome poultry is easy if you follow these guidelines.

Label and Package

- Check the sell-by date on the label (product dating is not a federal requirement), which indicates the last day the product should be sold; the product will still be fresh and wholesome if prepared and eaten within two days of this date.

- Package trays or bags should have very little or no liquid in the bottom.

- Avoid torn and leaking packages.

- Avoid packages that are stacked in the refrigerator case too high, as these packages are not being kept cool enough, and this shortens shelf life.

- Frozen poultry should be firm to the touch and free of freezer burn (light- or white-colored spots) and tears in packaging.

Odor and Appearance

- Check for a fresh odor (off odors can usually be detected through the plastic). If any unusual odors are detected, the product is not fresh.

- Select whole birds and cut-up pieces that are plump and meaty with smooth, moist-looking skin.

- Skinless boneless products should look plump and moist.

- The color of chicken skin doesn't indicate quality. Skin color ranges from yellow to white, depending on what the chicken was fed. Turkey should have cream-colored skin.

- The cut ends of poultry bones should be pink to red in color; if gray, the poultry is not fresh.

- Avoid poultry that has traces of feathers.

Handling with Care

- To prevent poultry from contaminating any foods in your grocery cart that will be eaten without cooking, put poultry in plastic bags and place them in the cart so that juices do not drip on other foods.

POULTRY STORAGE

Refrigerating

Uncooked Poultry: Tray-packed products and whole products packaged in bags should be stored in their original wrapping in the coldest part of refrigerator (40°F or below). Products wrapped in meat-market paper should be rinsed with cold water, patted dry with paper towels and repackaged in heavy-duty plastic bags, several layers of plastic wrap (place poultry in a dish or baking pan with sides, to prevent leakage on refrigerator shelves during storage) or food storage containers with tight-fitting lids. Refrigerate no longer than two days.

Cooked Poultry: Cover or wrap tightly and refrigerate no longer than two days. Chicken or turkey, giblets, stuffing and gravy should be stored in separate containers. Thoroughly reheat leftovers. Cover when reheating to retain moisture and ensure thorough heating in the center. Bring gravies and leftover marinade to a rolling boil and boil one minute before serving.

Freezing

Uncooked Poultry: Wrap tightly in moisture-vapor-resistant freezer wrap, heavy-duty plastic freezer bags or heavy-duty aluminum foil. Store giblets separately. Press as much air as possible out of the package before sealing it to prevent ice crystal formation and freezer burn. Mark the package with the date and contents and freeze. Cut-up chicken or turkey can be frozen for up to nine months. Whole chicken or turkey can be frozen for up to twelve months.

Cooked Poultry: Chicken or turkey, giblets, stuffing and gravy should be stored in separate containers. To freeze, wrap tightly in moisture-vapor–resistant freezer wrap, heavy-duty plastic bags or heavy-duty aluminum foil. Freeze for up to four months.

Thawing

Uncooked Poultry: Thaw frozen, uncooked chicken or turkey gradually in your refrigerator, never at room temperature on your countertop, because those temperatures provide the perfect environment for bacteria to grow. Place poultry in a dish or baking pan with sides, to prevent leakage on refrigerator shelves during thawing.

Thawing Time Guidelines

- **Whole Chicken:** Allow twenty-four hours for a three- to four-pound chicken.

- **Whole Turkey:** Allow twenty-four hours for each five pounds or use the following timetable:

    —1 to 2 days for eight to twelve pounds
    —2 to 3 for twelve to sixteen pounds
    —3 to 4 days for sixteen to twenty pounds
    —4 to 5 days for twenty to twenty-four pounds

- **Chicken or Turkey Cut-Up Parts:** Allow 3 to 9 hours for pieces.

Quick-thawing Guidelines

- **Cold-water Method:** Uncooked chicken and turkey may be safely thawed in cold water. Place poultry in its original wrap or in a sealable, heavy-duty plastic bag in cold water. Allow 30 minutes per pound to thaw, and change the water often. If not using immediately, store in refrigerator as directed above; do not freeze again.

- **Microwave Method:** Uncooked poultry can be thawed in the microwave oven following manufacturer's directions.

- **Cooked Poultry:** Thaw frozen, cooked chicken or turkey gradually in your refrigerator, never at room temperature on your countertop, because those temperatures provide the perfect environment for bacteria to grow. Allow three to nine hours for cubed, chopped or shredded pieces and up to twenty-four hours for whole pieces (bone in and boneless). You may also thaw cooked poultry in the microwave oven following manufacturer's directions.

CUTTING CHICKEN

For best results and for safety, it is important to use a sharp knife. Boning knives and poultry shears can be helpful. Poultry shears, also known as curved shears, are made of stainless steel and are about 9½ inches long with slightly curved blades and serrated edges. Unlike traditional scissors, poultry shears have a spring-loaded hinge design so they can exert the necessary force to cut through bone. The lower blade usually has a notch near the hinge for cutting through the smaller bones. After each use, wash with hot soapy water and dry very thoroughly with paper towels.

How to Slice Poultry Thinly

Have you ever been frustrated trying to slice raw chicken or turkey into thin, neat pieces? We have a solution for you! Freeze the poultry for about one hour or until firm and partially frozen. Using a sharp knife, slice it to the desired thickness across the grain. This method allows you to achieve picture-perfect slices every time.

How to Cut Up a Chicken

For best results and for safety, it is important to use a sharp knife. A boning knife has a slim, pointed blade and wide handle and works the best. Trim excess fat as you cut up the chicken. If you are not planning to brown the chicken pieces or if you are going to use the chicken in a stew or soup, you may wish to remove the skin.

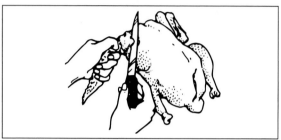

1 Place chicken, breast up, on cutting board. Remove wing from body by cutting into wing joint with a sharp knife, rolling knife to let the blade follow through at the curve of the joint as shown. Repeat with remaining wing.

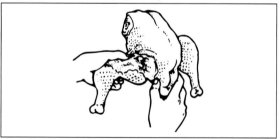

2 Cut off each leg by cutting skin between the thigh and body of the chicken; continue cutting through the meat between the tail and hip joint, cutting as closely as possible to the backbone. Bend leg back until hip joint pops out as shown.

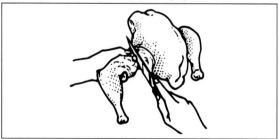

3 Continue cutting around bone and pulling leg from body until meat is separated from the bone as shown. Cut through remaining skin. Repeat on other side.

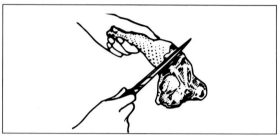

4 Separate thigh and drumstick by cutting about ⅛ inch from the fat line toward the drumstick side as shown. (A thin, white fat line runs crosswise at joint between drumstick and thigh.) Repeat with remaining leg.

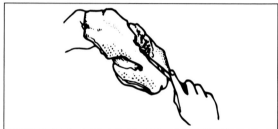

5 Separate back from breast by holding body, neck end down, and cutting downward along each side of backbone through the rib joints.

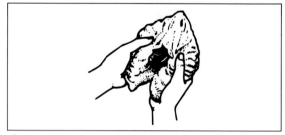

6 Placing breast with skin side down, cut just through the white cartilage at the V of the neck. Then bend breast halves back to pop out the keel bone; remove keel bone (for more detail, see step two on facing page). Using kitchen scissors or knife, cut breast into halves through wishbone; cut each breast half into halves.

How to Bone a Chicken Breast

Chicken breasts are available both whole and split. If starting with a split breast, simply pick up the following instructions at step three. For best results, use a boning knife with a 6-inch blade (see directions on facing page).

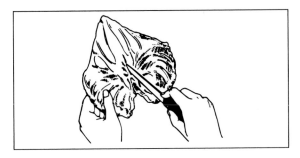

1 To bone a whole chicken breast, place chicken, skin side down, on cutting board. Cut through just the white cartilage at the V of the neck to expose the end of the keel bone (the dark bone at the center of the breast).

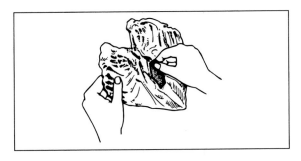

2 Bend breast halves back to pop out the keel bone. Loosen keel bone by running the tip of the index finger around both sides. Pull out bone in one or two pieces.

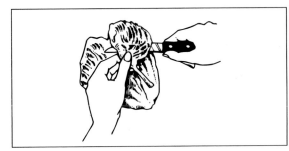

3 Working with one side of the breast, insert tip of knife under long rib bone. Cut rib cage away from breast, cutting through shoulder joint to remove entire rib cage. Repeat on other side.

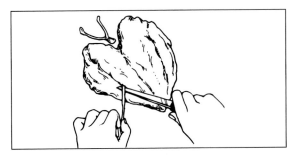

4 Turn chicken breast over and cut away wishbone. Slip knife under white tendons on either side of breast; loosen and pull out tendons. Remove skin if desired. Cut breast into halves; cut each breast half into halves if desired.

How to Carve Chicken and Turkey

For best results and for safety, it is important to use a sharp knife and a meat fork. A carving knife is your best bet, with a long, curved blade, and a meat fork is long-handled, and has two tines. Carve on a stable cutting surface, such as a cutting board. Carving is easier if the bird is allowed to stand for fifteen to twenty minutes before cutting. This resting period allows the meat to become more firm, creating smoother, more uniform slices.

1. Place bird, breast up, with legs to carver's right if right-handed and to the left if left-handed. Remove ties or skewers.

2. Gently pulling leg and thigh away from body, cut through joint between leg and body. Separate drumstick and thigh by cutting down through connecting joint.

■ **Special Note for Turkey:** Remove and separate drumstick and thigh as directed on page x. You can either serve drumsticks and thighs whole or carve them. Remove meat from drumstick by slicing at an angle. Slice thigh by cutting even slices parallel to the bone.

3. Make a deep horizontal cut into breast just above wing. Insert meat fork in top of breast as shown above, and, starting halfway up breast, carve thin slices down to the horizontal cut, working upward.

4. Repeat steps one through three on other side of bird.

FOOD SAFETY SAVVY

Food safety is of increasing concern to everyone, from manufacturing, processing and packaging to sanitary food practices in the supermarket and preparation in our homes. Why take precautions for food safety? Because microorganisms are always with us—on people and animals, in the air and water and on raw food.

Fact Versus Fiction: Bacteria, Food Spoilage and Food Poisoning

BACTERIA

Fiction: All bacteria are "bad."

Fact: Some bacteria are useful, such as the bacteria that cause fermentation in cheese and beer.

Fact: Some bacteria can cause foods to spoil, while others can cause food poisoning. The major difference between common spoilage and food poisoning are the temperatures at which bacteria thrive.

FOOD SPOILAGE

Fiction: If food doesn't smell or look bad, it's okay to eat it.

Fact: Bacteria that cause food to spoil can grow at refrigerator temperatures. Food spoilage can make food smell bad and various molds can form on the food, an obvious clue to throw it out. *However, several common bacteria can spoil food without leaving any telltale signs of odor or appearance.*

Fact: "When in Doubt, Throw It Out!" Getting sick isn't worth the money you may think you'll save by eating questionable food.

FOOD POISONING

Fiction: We've always put turkey leftovers out on the counter after dinner to cool and then to make sandwiches later on. Nobody has ever become sick, so why should I change the way I do things?

Fact: Never leave food out more than two hours; this will help to prevent bacterial growth. Most food-poisoning bacteria don't grow at refrigerator temperatures, but thrive at room temperatures (60° to 90°). Such bacteria are also called pathogens (among them are *Salmonella, Staphylococcus, Listeria, Clostridium perfringens* and *Clostridium botulinum*), and if consumed they may lead to illness, disease or death. *They cannot be detected by appearance, taste or smell.*

Salmonella: Salmonella can be contracted by the improper handling and cooking of chicken and turkey. *Salmonella* is very prevalent and can be found in water and soil, in the intestinal tract and on the skin of humans and all other animals and birds. Because it is so common, *Salmonella* may be present in foods such as raw chicken and turkey. When someone is infected with *Salmonella*, they develop flulike symptoms six to forty-eight hours after eating that can last two to seven days.

HANDLING FOOD SAFELY

The Basics

- Most food-poisoning bacteria can be controlled by cooking and refrigeration. So, the first food rule is to keep food adequately HOT or COLD. The second rule is to keep everything in the kitchen CLEAN, as most bacteria get into food through careless handling. Keep countertops, appliances, utensils and dishes sanitary by using hot, soapy water or other cleaners.

- Don't allow hot or cold foods to remain at room temperature for more than two hours, including preparation time; bacteria thrive in room-temperature and lukewarm food. A standard rule, recommended by the U.S. Department of Agriculture, is to **keep hot foods hot (above 140°)** and **cold foods cold (below 40°).**

- Once food has been cooked, keep it hot until serving time or refrigerate it as soon as possible. If it will not raise the refrigerator temperature above 45°, hot food can be placed immediately in the refrigerator. Food will cool more quickly in shallow containers (less than two inches deep), because it is spread out in a thin layer.

- Wash hands thoroughly with hot, soapy water. If you have any kind of skin cut or infection on your hands, avoid handling food or wear protective plastic gloves.

- Use paper towels when working with or cleaning up after preparing raw foods. If cloths or sponges are used, they should be laundered before they are used again.

Handling Raw Poultry

- Refer to poultry storage information (p. viii).

- Remove giblets (gizzard, heart and neck) if present. Rinse cavity. Rub cavity of bird lightly with salt, if desired. Do not salt cavity if bird is to be stuffed.

- Wash your hands in hot, soapy water before and after handling raw poultry.

- Do not use wooden cutting boards for raw poultry. Hard plastic cutting boards are less porous, safer, and easily cleaned or washed in a dishwasher. After preparing raw poultry, wash boards with a mixture of 2 teaspoons chlorine bleach and 1 teaspoon vinegar to 1 gallon of water. Wash knives in hot, soapy water.

- Use paper towels when working with or cleaning up after preparing raw poultry. If cloths or sponges are used, they should be laundered before they are used again.

- Be careful not to transfer potential bacteria from raw poultry to cooked poultry. For example, never carry raw poultry to the grill on a platter, then serve cooked poultry on the same unwashed platter. Do not cut up raw poultry and then use the same knife and cutting board to prepare other foods unless the utensils are washed thoroughly.

Stuffing Poultry

- Always stuff the poultry cavity loosely. This will allow the center to cook completely. The center of the stuffing should reach 165°. Never store leftover stuffing inside poultry, because it will not cool quickly enough; always store it in a separate container.

- Never stuff a chicken or turkey and then refrigerate or freeze it for later roasting; always stuff it just before it is to be cooked. This will help prevent any bacteria from contaminating the starchy dressing.

- Commercially stuffed poultry should be refrigerated immediately and cooked within two days.

Cooking Poultry

Always cook chicken and turkey to well done, never medium or rare. Don't interrupt cooking, as partial cooking may encourage bacterial growth before cooking is complete. The U.S. Department of Agriculture recommends using a meat thermometer when cooking whole chicken or turkey. The internal temperature should reach:

- **180°F** for whole birds with bone-in
- **170°F** for whole turkey breasts, bone-in pieces and boneless pieces
- **165°F** for stuffing

Thermometer Know-how

How to Insert a Thermometer

- **Whole Chicken or Turkey:** Insert meat thermometer so tip is in thickest part of inside thigh muscle and does not touch bone.

- **Whole Turkey Breast:** Insert meat thermometer so tip is in thickest part of breast muscle and does not touch bone.

- **Boneless Turkey Breast:** Insert meat thermometer so tip is in center of thickest part of breast muscle.

Types of Thermometers

Several types of meat thermometers are available, and it is important to purchase the right one for the job you want it to do.

- A *roast-yeast* thermometer (also called a meat and poultry or meat thermometer) is designed to be inserted and left in poultry or meat during cooking. The temperature gauge of this type of thermometer is protected by stainless steel, making it safe for use in the oven. This type of thermometer generally has both a temperature gauge and markings indicating doneness for various types of meat and poultry. We recommend determining doneness by the temperature gauge.

- An *instant-read* thermometer (also called instant or rapid-response thermometer) is designed to take an almost immediate temperature reading of the food being cooked (within one minute of insertion). This type of thermometer **is not designed to be left in the oven.** The temperature gauge of this thermometer is under a plastic cover—if left in the oven, the cover will melt and damage the gauge, resulting in inaccurate temperature readings.

Checking for Doneness without a Thermometer

Checking for doneness can be done without a meat thermometer, using a sharp knife or fork to cut into the muscle. Follow these guidelines:

- **Whole Chicken and Turkey:** Cook until juice of poultry is no longer pink when center of thigh is cut and drumstick moves easily when lifted or twisted.

- **Whole Turkey Breast:** Cook until juice of poultry is no longer pink when center is cut.

- **Cut-up Broiler-Fryers or Bone-in Pieces:** Cook until juice of poultry is no longer pink when centers of thickest pieces are cut.

- **Boneless Pieces:** Cook until juice of poultry is no longer pink when centers of thickest pieces are cut.

- **Small Pieces (as for stir-fry, fajitas or chicken tenders):** Cook until meat is no longer pink in center.

- **Ground:** Cook until meat is no longer pink.

- **Poultry Cooked in a Sauce or with Other Ingredients:** When checking for doneness, make certain you are checking that the juice of the poultry is running clear; do not confuse it with other liquids being cooked with the poultry.

All of our recipes include proper doneness indicators, which may include time, temperature, appearance or any combination of these.

NOTE: For a free copy of the brochure "A Quick Consumer Guide to Safe Food Handling," write to Publications, Room 1165-S, USDA, Washington, D.C. 20250.

GRILLING KNOW-HOW

Lighting Coals

- Light coals at least thirty minutes before cooking, to be sure proper temperature is reached. Most coals take between thirty and forty-five minutes to reach the proper temperature.

- When are the coals ready? In daylight, the coals should be completely covered with light gray ash. After dark, the coals will glow red.

Grill Rack

- Grease or oil the rack before lighting coals or turning gas on.

- Place the grill rack four to six inches above the coals or gas burners.

Cooking

- For even cooking, place meatier poultry pieces in the center of the grill rack and smaller pieces toward the edges, and turn pieces frequently.

- To retain poultry juices (and keep poultry from becoming dry), turn pieces with tongs instead of a fork.

- To prevent overbrowning or burning, brush sauces on during the last fifteen to twenty minutes of cooking, especially those containing tomato or sugar.

Food Safety

- Never serve cooked poultry on the same unwashed platter that held the raw poultry.

- Marinades and sauces left over from contact with raw poultry must be heated to boiling and boiled one minute before being served.

NUTRITION FACTS ABOUT POULTRY

	Calories	Protein (g)	Fat (g)	Cholesterol (mg)		Calories	Protein (g)	Fat (g)	Cholesterol (mg)
Chicken (3 ounces baked)*					**Turkey** (3 ounces baked)*				
WHOLE					**WHOLE**				
with skin	200	23	11.5	75	with skin	190	24	10.0	70
without skin	160	24	6.5	75	without skin	155	25	5.5	70
BREAST					**BREAST**				
with skin	165	25	6.5	70	with skin	180	25	8.0	70
without skin	140	26	3.0	70	without skin	140	26	3.5	65
THIGH					**THIGH**				
with skin	210	21	13.0	80	with skin	180	24	8.0	70
without skin	180	22	9.5	80	without skin	170	24	7.0	75
DRUMSTICK					**DRUMSTICK**				
with skin	185	23	9.5	80	with skin	180	24	8.0	70
without skin	145	24	5.0	80	without skin	170	24	7.0	75
WING					**WING**				
with skin	245	23	16.5	70	with skin	175	23	8.5	100
without skin	175	26	7.0	70	without skin	140	26	3.0	85
GROUND (regular)	200	24	11.0	80	**GROUND** (regular)	195	21	11.5	60

* Values listed for 3 ounces of baked poultry are rounded for simplicity. Based on USDA Handbook No. 8–5 (*Poultry Products*) and University of Minnesota Nutrition Data System.

SUBSTITUTING CHICKEN PARTS

Your favorite chicken pieces can be used in any of the recipes in this book calling for a 3 to 3½ pound bone-in cut-up broiler-fryer chicken. Substitute 2 to 2½ pounds bone-in breasts, thighs, drumsticks or wings for the cut-up broiler-fryer. If you substitute pieces that are thicker and meatier than the pieces the recipe calls for, the cooking time may be longer. Remember, while breasts, thighs and drumsticks may cost more per pound, they have a higher yield of meat.

MICROWAVING POULTRY

Arrange poultry pieces skin side up with thickest parts to outside edge in a dish large enough to hold pieces in single layer. Cover tightly and microwave as directed right. **Note:** Only use a **microwave meat thermometer** designed to remain in the oven during cooking. Regular meat thermometers could damage your oven or explode. Instant-read thermometers can be used to check temperatures of poultry after removal from the oven.

MICROWAVING POULTRY (SEE BASIC RECIPE INFORMATION, LEFT)

Type	Weight (pounds)	Power Level	Time
Chicken			
Broiler-fryer, cut up	3 to 3½	High	15 to 20 minutes, rotating dish ½ turn after 10 minutes, until juice of chicken is no longer pink when centers of thickest pieces are cut.
Breast halves, bone in, with skin	about 1¼	High	8 to 10 minutes, rotating dish ½ turn after 4 minutes, until juice of chicken is no longer pink when centers of thickest pieces are cut.
Breast halves, skinless boneless	about 1½	High	8 to 10 minutes, rotating dish ½ turn after 4 minutes, until juice of chicken is no longer pink when centers of thickest pieces are cut.
Wings	3 to 3½	High	12 to 15 minutes, rotating dish ½ turn after 6 minutes, until juice of chicken is no longer pink when centers of thickest pieces are cut.
Legs or thighs	2	High	16 to 19 minutes, rotating dish ½ turn after 10 minutes, until juice of chicken is no longer pink when centers of thickest pieces are cut.
Ground	1	High	6 to 8 minutes, stirring after 4 minutes, until chicken is no longer pink.
Rock Cornish Hens			
One	1 to 1½	High	10 to 13 minutes, turning over after 10 minutes, until thermometer reads 180°F and juice of hen is no longer pink when center of thigh is cut.
Two	2 to 3	High	15 to 20 minutes, turning over after 10 minutes, until thermometer reads 180°F and juice of hen is no longer pink when center of thigh is cut.
Turkey			
Boneless whole breast, **place skin side down**	4 to 5	High	10 minutes, rotating dish ½ turn until thermometer reads 170°F and juice of turkey is no longer pink when center is cut.
		Medium (50%)	40 to 50 minutes; turn breast over after 25 minutes, until thermometer reads 170°F and juice of turkey is no longer pink when center is cut.
Tenderloins	about 1½	High	8 to 10 minutes, rotating dish ½ turn after 4 minutes, until juice of turkey is no longer pink when centers of thickest pieces are cut.
Breast slices	1	High	3 to 5 minutes, rotating dish ½ turn after 2 minutes, until turkey is no longer pink in center.
Ground	1	High	6 to 8 minutes, stirring after 4 minutes, until turkey is no longer pink.

CHAPTER
1

The Whole Bird

It's wonderful to smell chicken or turkey roasting in the oven, the aroma making the whole house welcoming and cheerful. And, it's even better when it's time to eat the roasted bird! We've gathered delicious recipes that will add excitement to roasting chicken, turkey, and even Rock Cornish Hens. Sample Roast Chicken with Couscous and Chile Sauce, Asian Chicken with Kumquat Sauce or Spiced-rubbed Rock Cornish Hens. You'll appreciate our roasting chart which will tell you how to cook both stuffed and unstuffed birds, then you can turn to our section on stuffings and pick your favorite. Whether you'd like traditional or exotic recipes, the ones here will fill the bill.

Chicken with Wild Rice and Cranberry Stuffing
(page 4)

Herb-roasted Chicken with Lemon Rice

2 cups cooked rice

2 tablespoons chopped fresh parsley

1 tablespoon finely chopped fresh lemongrass or 1 teaspoon shredded lemon peel

1 teaspoon finely shredded lemon peel

3- to 3½-pound broiler-fryer chicken

1 package (3 ounces) cream cheese, softened

1 tablespoon chopped fresh or 1 teaspoon dried basil leaves

Heat oven to 375°. Mix rice, parsley, lemongrass and lemon peel. Fill wishbone area of chicken with rice mixture. Fold wings across back with tips touching. Fill body cavity lightly with rice mixture. Tie or skewer drumsticks to tail.

Place chicken, breast side up, on rack in shallow roasting pan. Mix cream cheese and basil. Loosen breast skin gently with fingers as far back as possible without tearing skin. Spread cream cheese mixture between breast meat and skin. Cover breast with skin. Insert meat thermometer so tip is in thickest part of inside thigh muscle and does not touch bone.

Roast uncovered 1 hour to 1 hour 30 minutes or until thermometer reads 180° and juice of chicken is no longer pink when center of thigh is cut. *6 servings.*

NUTRITION INFORMATION PER SERVING

1 serving		Percent of U.S. RDA	
Calories	355	Vitamin A	8%
Protein, g	30	Vitamin C	*
Carbohydrate, g	20	Calcium	4%
Fat, g	17	Iron	14%
Cholesterol, mg	100		
Sodium, mg	380		

Chicken with Potato Stuffing

Old-fashioned potato stuffing takes on Latin-American flavor with sweet fruit and sausage. You can use either instant or fresh mashed potatoes in this recipe.

8 ounces bulk hot or regular pork, Italian or chorizo sausage

½ cup chopped onion (about 1 medium)

2 cups hot mashed potatoes

1½ cups soft bread crumbs (about 2½ slices bread)

½ cup chopped dried peaches or apricots

1 tablespoon chopped fresh or 1 teaspoon dried oregano leaves

¾ teaspoon salt

⅛ teaspoon pepper

1 egg, beaten

3- to 3½-pound broiler-fryer chicken

Heat oven to 375°. Cook sausage and onion in 10-inch skillet over medium heat, stirring frequently, until sausage is brown; drain and remove from heat. Stir in remaining ingredients except chicken.

Fill wishbone area of chicken with stuffing. Fold wings across back with tips touching. Fill body cavity lightly with stuffing. (Place any remaining stuffing in small ungreased baking dish; cover and refrigerate. Place in oven with chicken the last 30 minutes of roasting.) Tie or skewer drumsticks to tail. Place chicken, breast side up, on rack in shallow roasting pan. Insert meat thermometer so tip is in thickest part of inside thigh muscle and does not touch bone.

Roast uncovered about 1 hour 30 minutes or until thermometer reads 180° and juice of chicken is no longer pink when center of thigh is cut. *6 servings.*

NUTRITION INFORMATION PER SERVING

1 serving		Percent of U.S. RDA	
Calories	565	Vitamin A	10%
Protein, g	41	Vitamin C	2%
Carbohydrate, g	42	Calcium	8%
Fat, g	26	Iron	22%
Cholesterol, mg	150		
Sodium, mg	1100		

Chicken with Wild Rice and Cranberry Stuffing

¾ cup uncooked wild rice

1¾ cups chicken broth

½ cup chopped onion (about 1 medium)

½ cup thinly sliced celery (about 1 medium stalk)

½ cup coarsely chopped cranberries

¼ cup orange juice

2 tablespoons packed brown sugar

1 teaspoon grated orange peel

½ teaspoon ground nutmeg

⅓ cup coarsely chopped pecans or slivered almonds, toasted

3- to 3½-pound broiler-fryer chicken

Place wild rice in wire strainer. Run cold water through rice, lifting rice with fingers to clean thoroughly. Heat wild rice and broth to boiling in 1½-quart saucepan, stirring once or twice; reduce heat. Cover and simmer 30 minutes, stirring occasionally. Stir in remaining ingredients except pecans and chicken. Cover and simmer 10 to 20 minutes longer, stirring occasionally, until liquid is absorbed and vegetables are just tender. Stir in pecans.

Heat oven to 375°. Fill wishbone area of chicken with stuffing. Fold wings across back with tips touching. Fill body cavity lightly with stuffing. (Place any remaining stuffing in small ungreased baking dish; cover and refrigerate. Place in oven with chicken the last 30 minutes of roasting.) Tie or skewer drumsticks to tail. Place chicken, breast side up, on rack in shallow roasting pan. Insert meat thermometer so tip is in thickest part of inside thigh muscle and does not touch bone.

Roast uncovered about 1 hour 30 minutes or until thermometer reads 180° and juice of chicken is no longer pink when center of thigh is cut. *6 servings.*

NUTRITION INFORMATION PER SERVING

1 serving		Percent of U.S. RDA	
Calories	415	Vitamin A	2%
Protein, g	33	Vitamin C	*
Carbohydrate, g	35	Calcium	6%
Fat, g	16	Iron	14%
Cholesterol, mg	85		
Sodium, mg	320		

Rice-stuffed Chicken

⅓ cup margarine or butter, melted

1 teaspoon salt

1 teaspoon ground ginger

½ teaspoon grated lemon peel

¼ teaspoon garlic powder

1½ cups cooked brown or white rice

1 cup chopped apple (about 1 medium)

¼ cup chopped nuts

½ cup chopped prunes

½ cup chopped dried apricots

¼ cup chopped celery

3- to 3½-pound broiler-fryer chicken

2 tablespoons margarine or butter, melted

¼ teaspoon paprika

Heat oven to 375°. Mix ⅓ cup margarine, the salt, ginger, lemon peel and garlic powder; toss with rice, apple, nuts, prunes, apricots and celery. Fill wishbone area of chicken with rice mixture. Fold wings across back with tips touching. Fill body cavity lightly with remaining rice mixture. Tie or skewer drumsticks to tail.

Place chicken, breast side up, on rack in shallow roasting pan. Mix 2 tablespoons margarine and the paprika; brush on chicken.

Roast uncovered 1 to 1½ hours or until thermometer reads 180° and juice of chicken is no longer pink when center of thigh is cut. *6 servings.*

NUTRITION INFORMATION PER SERVING

1 serving		Percent of U.S. RDA	
Calories	505	Vitamin A	32%
Protein, g	30	Vitamin C	*
Carbohydrate, g	31	Calcium	4%
Fat, g	29	Iron	16%
Cholesterol, mg	85		
Sodium, mg	730		

Autumn Roast Chicken

3- to 3½-pound broiler-fryer chicken

3 pounds buttercup or acorn squash, cut into 1-inch rings or slices

6 medium onions, cut in half

½ cup (1 stick) margarine or butter, melted

¼ cup lemon juice

2 tablespoons honey

2 teaspoons dried rosemary leaves, crushed

1 clove garlic, finely chopped

Heat oven to 375°. Fold wings of chicken across back with tips touching. Tie or skewer drumsticks to tail. Place chicken, breast side up, on rack in shallow roasting pan. Arrange squash and onions around chicken. Mix remaining ingredients; brush on chicken and vegetables. Insert meat thermometer in chicken so tip is in thickest part of inside thigh muscle and does not touch bone.

Roast uncovered about 1 hour 30 minutes, brushing chicken and vegetables several times with remaining margarine mixture, until thermometer reads 180°, juice of chicken is no longer pink when center of thigh is cut and squash is tender. *6 servings.*

NUTRITION INFORMATION PER SERVING

1 serving		Percent of U.S. RDA	
Calories	510	Vitamin A	94%
Protein, g	30	Vitamin C	20%
Carbohydrate, g	34	Calcium	8%
Fat, g	28	Iron	14%
Cholesterol, mg	85		
Sodium, mg	260		

Stuffing Know-How

Serving chicken or turkey with stuffing, or "dressing," is an American tradition. But why wait until holiday time to make stuffing? Stuffing can be enjoyed at any time, and not just with whole birds! Try serving it as a side dish, instead of rice or potatoes, to chicken or turkey pieces. Our mix of traditional stuffings and those with great new flavor combinations will whet your appetite to make them a part of your meals all the time, not just during the holidays.

Stuffing Savvy

Selecting Bread

- Traditionally, white bread is used, but you can use breads such as whole grain, sourdough, rye or corn bread.
- Day-old or stale bread works best for stuffing, because it is easier to cut into cubes and it does not become as compact and soft during baking as does very fresh bread.

How Much Stuffing Should I Use?

- Allow ½ cup stuffing per pound of poultry when stuffing the cavity.

How Do I Stuff Poultry?

- Always stuff poultry just before cooking. This will keep any bacteria in the raw poultry from contaminating the starchy dressing.

- Always stuff the poultry cavity loosely. This will allow it to expand and thoroughly cook. **The center of the stuffing inside poultry should reach 165°.**

- If you have more stuffing than the cavity can hold, spoon the extra into a greased casserole and refrigerate until about thirty minutes before poultry is done. Cover and bake in the same oven with the poultry until hot, about thirty to forty-five minutes.

How Do I Store Stuffing?

- Never store leftover stuffing inside poultry because it will not cool quickly enough, which could allow bacteria to start growing; always store it in a separate, shallow container (less than two inches deep).

Traditional Bread Stuffing	Directions	Additional Ingredients or Substitutions
1½ cups chopped celery *¾ cup chopped onion* *½ cup margarine or butter* *9 cups soft bread cubes or corn bread cubes* *1½ teaspoons chopped fresh or ½ teaspoon dried sage leaves, crumbled* *1½ teaspoons chopped fresh or ½ teaspoon dried thyme leaves* *1 teaspoon salt* *⅛ teaspoon pepper*	Cook and stir celery and onion in margarine about 2 minutes. Remove from heat. Stir in remaining ingredients; toss. About 9 cups stuffing.	■ ½ to 1 cup chopped, cooked giblets. Add with remaining ingredients. ■ 1 (8 ounce) can oysters, drained and chopped. Add with remaining ingredients. ■ 1 cup sliced fresh mushrooms. Cook with celery and onion. ■ ½ pound bulk pork or Italian sausage, browned and well drained. Add with remaining ingredients.

Whole Grain Apple-Cranberry Stuffing	Directions	Additional Ingredients or Substitutions
¾ cup chopped onion ½ cup chopped celery ½ cup margarine or butter 9 cups soft whole grain bread cubes 2½ cups chopped apples ½ cup dried cranberries 1½ teaspoons chopped fresh or ½ teaspoon dried sage leaves, crumbled 1½ teaspoons chopped fresh or ½ teaspoon dried thyme leaves 1 teaspoon salt ⅛ teaspoon pepper ½ cup chicken broth or water	Cook and stir onion and celery in margarine about 2 minutes. Remove from heat. Stir in remaining ingredients except chicken broth; mix well. Add chicken broth; toss. About 9 cups stuffing.	■ ¼ teaspoon cinnamon and a dash of nutmeg. Add with remaining ingredients. ■ Substitute dried cherries or raisins for the dried cranberries.

Apricot–Wild Rice Stuffing	Directions	Additional Ingredients or Substitutions
1¼ cups hot water 1 cup cooked wild rice ½ cup chopped, toasted pecans ½ cup chopped dried apricots ¼ cup margarine or butter, melted 1 large onion, chopped 1 package (8 ounces) herb stuffing mix	Mix all ingredients in large bowl. Stir to blend well. About 8 cups stuffing.	■ Substitute cooked brown or white rice for the wild rice. ■ Substitute softened bulgur or kasha, cooked barley, cooked quinoa or cooked wheat berries for the wild rice. ■ Substitute chopped walnut or almonds for the pecans.

(Recipes continue on following pages)

STUFFING KNOW-HOW (*continued*)

Southwest Stuffing	Directions	Additional Ingredients or Substitutions
1 cup chopped chayote squash (about 1 small) *4 jalapeño chiles, seeded and finely chopped* *2 cloves garlic, finely chopped* *1 cup chopped onion* *¾ cup margarine or butter* *1 tablespoon finely chopped fresh cilantro or parsley* *1 teaspoon salt* *1½ teaspoons chopped fresh or ½ teaspoon dried thyme leaves* *1½ teaspoons chopped fresh or ½ teaspoon dried sage leaves, crumbled* *9 cups ½-inch corn bread cubes* *1 cup chopped pecans* *1 cup chicken broth or water*	Cook and stir chayote, chiles, garlic and onion in margarine in Dutch oven until chayote is tender. Stir in cilantro, salt, thyme and sage until well blended. Remove from heat. Stir in corn bread and pecans; mix well. Add broth; toss. About 9 cups stuffing.	■ Substitute chopped zucchini for the chayote. ■ Substitute pine nuts for the pecans. ■ Substitute ½ cup chopped green or red bell pepper for the jalapeños.

Barley-Carrot Stuffing	Directions	Additional Ingredients or Substitutions
½ cup chopped celery *¼ cup chopped onion* *2 tablespoons margarine or butter* *2 cups cooked barley* *1⅓ cups shredded carrot* *⅓ cup chopped walnuts* *½ teaspoon salt* *⅛ teaspoon pepper* *4 slices bacon, crisply cooked and crumbled*	Cook and stir celery and onion in margarine in 10-inch skillet about 2 minutes. Remove from heat. Stir in remaining ingredients; toss. About 4 cups stuffing. (NOTE: All recipes can be halved.)	■ Substitute cooked rice, couscous or orzo pasta for the barley. ■ Substitute shredded zucchini for the carrot. ■ Substitute chopped cooked ham for the bacon.

How to Roast Chicken and Turkey

Remove giblets (gizzard, heart and neck) if present. Rinse the cavity. Rub cavity of bird lightly with salt, if desired. Do not salt cavity if bird is to be stuffed. If stuffing bird, do so just before roasting as this will keep any bacteria in the raw poultry from contaminating the starchy dressing. Allow ½ cup stuffing per pound of poultry. Fill wishbone area with stuffing first. For turkey, fasten neck skin to back with skewer (not necessary for chicken). Fold wings across back with tips touching. Fill cavity lightly. (**Do not pack**— stuffing will expand while cooking). For chicken, tie or skewer drumsticks to tail. For turkey, tuck drumsticks under band of skin at tail, or tie or skewer to tail.

Place bird, breast side up, on rack in shallow roasting pan. Brush with melted margarine or butter. Do not add water. Do not cover. Follow table below for approximate roasting time. Insert ovenproof meat thermometer (not instant-read type) so tip is in thickest part of inside thigh muscle and does not touch bone. For turkey, place a tent of aluminum foil loosely over turkey when it begins to turn golden-brown. When bird is two-thirds done, cut band or remove tie or skewer holding legs.

Roast until thermometer temperature reaches 180°F and juice is no longer pink when center of thigh is cut. The drumstick should move easily when lifted and twisted. If the bird is stuffed, the center of the stuffing should reach an internal temperature of 165°F (this includes commercially stuffed poultry). When done, remove bird from the oven and let stand about 15 minutes for easiest carving.

TIMETABLE FOR ROASTING CHICKEN AND TURKEY

Poultry Type (whole)	Uncooked Weight (pounds)	Oven Temperature	Approximate Roasting Time (hours)*
Chicken (not stuffed)	3 to 3½	375°	1¾ to 2
Chicken (stuffed)	3 to 3½	325°	2 to 2½
Turkey (not stuffed)	6 to 8	325°	2¼ to 3¼
	8 to 12	325°	3 to 4
	12 to 16	325°	3½ to 4½
	16 to 20	325°	4 to 5
	20 to 24	325°	4½ to 5½
Turkey (stuffed)	6 to 8	325°	3 to 3½
	8 to 12	325°	3½ to 4½
	12 to 16	325°	4 to 5
	16 to 20	325°	4½ to 5½
	20 to 24	325°	5 to 6½

* Roasting times will be affected by types of oven, actual oven temperature and shape and tenderness of bird. Begin checking turkey doneness about 1 hour before end of recommended roasting time. For commercially stuffed turkeys, follow package directions very carefully; do not use this timetable.

Roast Chicken with Couscous and Chile Sauce

This tasty dish is adapted from a Moroccan favorite. Typically, Moroccans blend the Chile Sauce into the couscous as they eat so the sweetness of the couscous mixture mellows the fiery sauce.

Chile Sauce (right)
3- to 3½-pound broiler-fryer chicken
1 cup chicken broth
½ cup raisins
1 tablespoon margarine or butter
½ teaspoon chile powder
½ teaspoon ground ginger
½ teaspoon ground cumin
¼ teaspoon salt
1 can (15 ounces) garbanzo beans, undrained
1 can (8 ounces) stewed tomatoes, undrained
1 cup uncooked couscous

Prepare Chile Sauce. Heat oven to 375°. Fold wings of chicken across back with tips touching. Tie or skewer drumsticks to tail. Place chicken, breast side up, on rack in shallow roasting pan. Insert meat thermometer so tip is in thickest part of inside thigh muscle and does not touch bone. Roast uncovered about 1 hour 30 minutes or until thermometer reads 180° and juice of chicken is no longer pink when center of thigh is cut.

Just before serving, heat remaining ingredients except couscous and Green Chile Sauce to boiling in 2-quart saucepan. Stir in couscous; remove from heat. Cover and let stand about 5 minutes or until liquid is absorbed. Serve chicken and couscous mixture with sauce. *6 servings.*

CHILE SAUCE

¼ cup coarsely chopped onion (about 1 small)
¼ cup parsley sprigs
1 to 2 tablespoons coarsely chopped canned jalapeño chiles
1 tablespoon lemon juice
1 teaspoon ground cumin
1 teaspoon ground coriander
1 can (8 ounces) stewed tomatoes, undrained

Place all ingredients in blender or food processor. Cover and blend, or process, just until chunky. Cover and refrigerate until serving time.

NUTRITION INFORMATION PER SERVING

1 serving		Percent of U.S. RDA	
Calories	535	Vitamin A	14%
Protein, g	38	Vitamin C	20%
Carbohydrate, g	58	Calcium	8%
Fat, g	17	Iron	28%
Cholesterol, mg	85		
Sodium, mg	650		

Sweet Roasted Chicken

Simmered chicken-in-a-pot tastes wonderfully sweet when you use spices and fruit instead of the traditional herbs and vegetables.

3- to 3½-pound broiler-fryer chicken

1 can (15¼ ounces) pineapple chunks, drained and juice reserved

½ cup dried apricot halves

½ cup orange juice

3 medium sweet potatoes, peeled and cut into 1½-inch pieces (about 4 cups)

¼ cup rum or orange juice

1 tablespoon packed brown sugar

½ teaspoon ground ginger

½ teaspoon ground cinnamon

⅛ teaspoon salt

2 tablespoons cold water

1 tablespoon cornstarch

Heat oven to 375°. Fold wings of chicken across back with tips touching. Tie or skewer drumsticks to tail. Place chicken, breast side up, in Dutch oven. Insert meat thermometer so tip is in thickest part of inside thigh muscle and does not touch bone. Arrange pineapple and apricots around chicken. Pour orange juice over chicken. Cover and bake 1 hour 15 minutes.

Add sweet potatoes to Dutch oven. Cover and bake 30 to 45 minutes longer or until thermometer reads 180° and juice of chicken is no longer pink when center of thigh is cut. Remove chicken from Dutch oven to warm platter. Remove sweet potatoes, pineapple and apricots from Dutch oven, using slotted spoon, and arrange around chicken; keep warm.

Skim fat from drippings in Dutch oven; reserve ½ cup drippings. Drain remaining drippings from Dutch oven. Return reserved ½ cup drippings to Dutch oven. Stir in reserved pineapple juice, the rum, brown sugar, ginger, cinnamon and salt. Heat to boiling over medium heat. Mix water and cornstarch; stir into pineapple juice mixture. Heat to boiling, stirring constantly. Boil and stir 1 minute until mixture thickens. Serve sauce with chicken, sweet potatoes, pineapple and apricots. *6 servings.*

NUTRITION INFORMATION PER SERVING

1 serving		*Percent of U.S. RDA*	
Calories	450	Vitamin A	100%
Protein, g	29	Vitamin C	20%
Carbohydrate, g	57	Calcium	6%
Fat, g	12	Iron	20%
Cholesterol, mg	85		
Sodium, mg	170		

Chicken with Fennel

This easy herb butter calls for only a few ingredients but delivers an abundance of flavor.

> *3- to 3½-pound broiler-fryer chicken*
>
> *¼ cup (½ stick) margarine or butter, softened*
>
> *1½ tablespoons chopped fresh or 1½ teaspoons dried basil leaves*
>
> *1 tablespoon chopped fresh parsley or 1 teaspoon dried parsley flakes*
>
> *½ teaspoon fennel seed*
>
> *⅛ teaspoon pepper*

Heat oven to 375°. Fold wings of chicken across back with tips touching. Tie or skewer drumsticks to tail. Place chicken, breast side up, on rack in shallow roasting pan. Insert meat thermometer so tip is in thickest part of inside thigh muscle and does not touch bone.

Mix remaining ingredients. Loosen breast skin gently with fingers as far back as possible without tearing skin. Spread margarine mixture between breast meat and skin. Cover breast with skin.

Roast uncovered about 1 hour 30 minutes or until thermometer reads 180° and juice of chicken is no longer pink when center of thigh is cut. *6 servings.*

NUTRITION INFORMATION PER SERVING

1 serving		Percent of U.S. RDA	
Calories	280	Vitamin A	12%
Protein, g	27	Vitamin C	*
Carbohydrate, g	0	Calcium	2%
Fat, g	19	Iron	10%
Cholesterol, mg	85		
Sodium, mg	160		

Spanish Chicken with Vegetables and Olives

> *3- to 3½-pound broiler-fryer chicken*
>
> *¼ cup (½ stick) margarine or butter, melted*
>
> *3 medium tomatoes, cut into wedges*
>
> *2 medium green bell peppers, cut into rings*
>
> *2 medium onions, sliced*
>
> *1 clove garlic, finely chopped*
>
> *¼ pound fully cooked smoked ham, cut up (1 cup)*
>
> *8 pitted ripe olives, cut in half*
>
> *1 teaspoon salt*
>
> *¼ teaspoon pepper*
>
> *Hot cooked rice, if desired*

Heat oven to 375°. Fold wings of chicken across back with tips touching. Tie or skewer drumsticks to tail. Brush with margarine. Place chicken, breast side up, in ovenproof Dutch oven.

Roast uncovered 1 to 1½ hours, brushing with drippings occasionally, until thermometer reads 180° and juice of chicken is no longer pink when center of thigh is cut. Add tomatoes, bell peppers, onions, garlic, ham and olives. Sprinkle chicken and vegetables with salt and pepper.

Cover and bake about 20 minutes or until bell pepper is tender. Place chicken on serving platter. Arrange vegetables and ham around chicken. Serve with rice. *6 to 8 servings.*

NUTRITION INFORMATION PER SERVING

1 serving		Percent of U.S. RDA	
Calories	370	Vitamin A	18%
Protein, g	32	Vitamin C	20%
Carbohydrate, g	9	Calcium	4%
Fat, g	23	Iron	14%
Cholesterol, mg	95		
Sodium, mg	750		

Southwest Roast Chicken

A robust Tex-Mex chicken that's a zesty change of pace.

3- to 3½-pound broiler-fryer chicken

¼ cup (½ stick) margarine or butter, melted

2 teaspoons chopped fresh or ½ teaspoon dried sage leaves, crumbled

1 teaspoon chile powder

½ teaspoon ground coriander

¼ teaspoon ground red pepper (cayenne)

2 cloves garlic, finely chopped

Heat oven to 375°. Fold wings of chicken across back with tips touching. Tie or skewer drumsticks to tail. Place chicken, breast side up, on rack in shallow roasting pan. Insert meat thermometer so tip is in thickest part of inside thigh muscle and does not touch bone.

Roast uncovered 30 minutes. Mix remaining ingredients; brush generously on chicken. Roast uncovered about 1 hour longer, brushing once or twice with margarine mixture, until thermometer reads 180° and juice of chicken is no longer pink when center of thigh is cut. *6 servings.*

NUTRITION INFORMATION PER SERVING

1 serving		Percent of U.S. RDA	
Calories	285	Vitamin A	14%
Protein, g	27	Vitamin C	*
Carbohydrate, g	1	Calcium	2%
Fat, g	19	Iron	10%
Cholesterol, mg	85		
Sodium, mg	170		

Tarragon Chicken

3- to 3½-pound broiler-fryer chicken

¼ cup (½ stick) margarine or butter, melted

1 tablespoon chopped fresh or 1 teaspoon dried tarragon leaves

¾ teaspoon lemon pepper

½ teaspoon onion powder

¼ teaspoon garlic powder

Heat oven to 375°. Fold wings of chicken across back with tips touching. Tie or skewer drumsticks to tail. Place chicken, breast side up, on rack in shallow roasting pan. Insert meat thermometer so tip is in thickest part of inside thigh muscle and does not touch bone. Mix remaining ingredients; brush generously on chicken.

Roast uncovered about 1 hour 30 minutes, brushing 2 or 3 times with remaining margarine mixture, until thermometer reads 180° and juice of chicken is no longer pink when center of thigh is cut. *6 servings.*

NUTRITION INFORMATION PER SERVING

1 serving		Percent of U.S. RDA	
Calories	285	Vitamin A	12%
Protein, g	27	Vitamin C	*
Carbohydrate, g	1	Calcium	2%
Fat, g	19	Iron	10%
Cholesterol, mg	85		
Sodium, mg	160		

Asian Chicken with Kumquat Sauce

This tantalizing roast chicken borrows its flavor from Asian seasoning. While roasting, it's basted with sherry and soy sauce, then served with piquant Kumquat Sauce.

3- to 3½-pound broiler-fryer chicken

3 tablespoons sherry or orange juice

2 tablespoons soy sauce

½ teaspoon garlic powder

Kumquat Sauce (right)

Heat oven to 375°. Fold wings of chicken across back with tips touching. Tie or skewer drumsticks to tail. Place chicken, breast side up, on rack in shallow roasting pan. Insert meat thermometer so tip is in thickest part of inside thigh muscle and does not touch bone.

Roast uncovered 45 minutes. Mix sherry, soy sauce and garlic powder; brush on chicken. Roast uncovered about 45 minutes longer, brushing with remaining sherry mixture, until thermometer reads 180° and juice of chicken is no longer pink when center of thigh is cut. Serve chicken with Kumquat Sauce. *6 servings.*

KUMQUAT SAUCE

⅓ cup thinly sliced preserved kumquats (from 10-ounce jar) or chopped dried peaches or apricots

½ cup orange juice

3 tablespoons orange marmalade

1 tablespoon lemon juice

¼ teaspoon ground ginger

1 tablespoon cold water

2 teaspoons cornstarch

2 tablespoons slivered almonds, toasted

1 tablespoon orange-flavored liqueur, if desired

Remove seeds from kumquats; reserve kumquats. Mix orange juice, orange marmalade, lemon juice and ginger in 1-quart saucepan. (If using dried peaches or apricots, add them to saucepan.) Heat to boiling. Mix water and cornstarch; stir into orange juice mixture. Heat to boiling, stirring constantly. Boil and stir about 1 minute or until thickened. Stir in kumquats, almonds and liqueur.

TO GRILL: Prepare chicken as directed. Prepare grill, arranging coals around edge of firebox. Place drip pan under grilling area. Cover and grill chicken, breast side up, 4 to 6 inches from medium coals 45 minutes. Mix sherry, soy sauce and garlic powder; brush on chicken. Cover and grill about 45 minutes longer, brushing once or twice with sherry mixture, until thermometer reads 180° and juice of chicken is no longer pink when center of thigh is cut. Discard any remaining sherry mixture.

NUTRITION INFORMATION PER SERVING

1 serving		Percent of U.S. RDA	
Calories	295	Vitamin A	4%
Protein, g	28	Vitamin C	4%
Carbohydrate, g	17	Calcium	4%
Fat, g	13	Iron	12%
Cholesterol, mg	85		
Sodium, mg	420		

Right: Asian Chicken with Kumquat Sauce

Caesar Chicken

3- to 3½-pound broiler-fryer chicken

½ cup caesar salad dressing (not creamy type)

Heat oven to 375°. Fold wings of chicken across back with tips touching. Tie or skewer drumsticks to tail. Place chicken, breast side up, on rack in shallow roasting pan. Insert meat thermometer so tip is in thickest part of inside thigh muscle and does not touch bone. Brush chicken with ¼ cup dressing.

Roast uncovered about 1½ hours, brushing 2 or 3 times with remaining dressing, until thermometer reads 180° and juice of chicken is no longer pink when center of thigh is cut. *6 servings.*

NUTRITION INFORMATION PER SERVING

1 serving		Percent of U.S. RDA	
Calories	325	Vitamin A	2%
Protein, g	27	Vitamin C	*
Carbohydrate, g	2	Calcium	2%
Fat, g	23	Iron	8%
Cholesterol, mg	85		
Sodium, mg	280		

Thyme-baked Chicken with Vegetables

3- to 3½-pound broiler-fryer chicken

6 medium carrots, cut into 1-inch pieces

4 medium stalks celery, cut into 1-inch pieces

3 medium baking potatoes, cut into 1½-inch pieces or 9 new red potatoes, halved

2 medium onions, cut into wedges

2 tablespoons margarine or butter, melted

4 teaspoons chopped fresh or 1 teaspoon dried thyme leaves

Heat oven to 375°. Fold wings of chicken across back with tips touching. Tie or skewer drumsticks to tail. Place chicken, breast side up, in shallow roasting pan. Insert meat thermometer so tip is in thickest part of inside thigh muscle and does not touch bone. Roast uncovered 45 minutes.

Arrange carrots, celery, potatoes and onions around chicken. Mix margarine and thyme; drizzle over chicken and vegetables. Cover and bake 45 to 60 minutes or until thermometer reads 180° and juice of chicken is no longer pink when center of thigh is cut and vegetables are tender. *6 servings.*

NUTRITION INFORMATION PER SERVING

1 serving		Percent of U.S. RDA	
Calories	360	Vitamin A	100%
Protein, g	30	Vitamin C	10%
Carbohydrate, g	29	Calcium	6%
Fat, g	14	Iron	18%
Cholesterol, mg	85		
Sodium, mg	380		

Thyme-baked Chicken with Vegetables

Tomatillo-sauced Chicken

Tomatillos, also called Mexican green tomatoes, are covered with a thin, paperlike brown husk that must be peeled away before you use them.

3- to 3½-pound broiler-fryer chicken

1 cup chopped tomatillos or roma (plum) tomatoes

¼ cup orange juice

2 tablespoons dry white wine or orange juice

½ teaspoon ground cumin

⅛ teaspoon salt

⅛ teaspoon pepper

½ small onion, cut into fourths

1 clove garlic

3 tablespoons margarine or butter

1 tablespoon chopped fresh or 1 teaspoon dried cilantro leaves

Heat oven to 375°. Fold wings of chicken across back with tips touching. Tie or skewer drumsticks to tail. Place chicken, breast side up, on rack in shallow roasting pan. Insert meat thermometer so tip is in thickest part of inside thigh muscle and does not touch bone. Roast uncovered about 1 hour 30 minutes or until thermometer reads 180° and juice of chicken is no longer pink when center of thigh is cut.

Meanwhile, place remaining ingredients except margarine and cilantro in blender or food processor. Cover and blend on medium speed about 20 seconds, or process, until very finely chopped. Heat tomatillo mixture to boiling in 1-quart saucepan; reduce heat. Simmer uncovered about 10 minutes, stirring occasionally, until slightly reduced. Beat in margarine, 1 tablespoon at a time, until melted. Stir in cilantro. Spoon some of the sauce over chicken. Serve remaining sauce. *6 servings.*

TO GRILL: Prepare chicken as directed. Prepare grill, arranging coals around edge of firebox. Place drip pan under grilling area. Cover and grill chicken, breast side up, 4 to 6 inches from medium coals about 1 hour 30 minutes or until thermometer reads 180° and juice of chicken is no longer pink when center of thigh is cut.

NUTRITION INFORMATION PER SERVING

1 serving		*Percent of U.S. RDA*	
Calories	275	Vitamin A	12%
Protein, g	27	Vitamin C	6%
Carbohydrate, g	4	Calcium	2%
Fat, g	17	Iron	10%
Cholesterol, mg	85		
Sodium, mg	190		

Chicken with Orange Glaze

This quick honey-orange glaze is an adaptation of the more time-consuming classic French orange sauce.

3- to 3½-pound broiler-fryer chicken

½ cup honey

2 tablespoons orange juice

1 tablespoon lemon juice

¼ teaspoon ground nutmeg

Heat oven to 375°. Fold wings of chicken across back with tips touching. Tie or skewer drumsticks to tail. Place chicken, breast side up, on rack in shallow roasting pan. Insert meat thermometer so tip is in thickest part of inside thigh muscle and does not touch bone.

Roast uncovered 1 hour 15 minutes. Mix remaining ingredients; reserve half of the orange mixture. Brush some of remaining orange mixture on chicken. Roast uncovered about 15 minutes longer, brushing once or twice with remaining orange mixture, until thermometer reads 180° and juice of chicken is no longer pink when center of thigh is cut. Serve chicken with reserved orange juice mixture. *6 servings.*

TO GRILL: Prepare chicken as directed. Prepare grill, arranging coals around edge of firebox. Place drip pan under grilling area. Cover and grill chicken, breast side up, 4 to 6 inches from medium coals 1 hour 15 minutes. Mix remaining ingredients; reserve half of the orange mixture. Brush some of remaining orange mixture on chicken. Cover and grill about 15 minutes longer, brushing once or twice with remaining orange mixture, until thermometer reads 180° and juice of chicken is no longer pink when center of thigh is cut.

NUTRITION INFORMATION PER SERVING

1 serving		Percent of U.S. RDA	
Calories	310	Vitamin A	2%
Protein, g	27	Vitamin C	*
Carbohydrate, g	24	Calcium	2%
Fat, g	12	Iron	8%
Cholesterol, mg	85		
Sodium, mg	75		

Roast Turkey with Cherry-Rye Stuffing

8- to 10-pound turkey

1 cup dried cherries or cranberries

1 cup water

3 tablespoons margarine or butter

1 cup chopped onion (about 1 large)

½ cup chopped celery (about 1 medium stalk)

1 tablespoon chopped fresh or 1 teaspoon dried sage leaves, crumbled

¼ teaspoon salt

7 cups light rye or whole wheat stuffing cubes

1 cup chopped pecans, toasted

1 cup chicken broth

Margarine or butter, melted

Heat oven to 325°. Prepare turkey as directed on page 9. Heat cherries and water to boiling in 1½-quart saucepan; reduce heat. Simmer uncovered 5 minutes. Thoroughly drain cherries, pressing out as much liquid as possible; reserve cherries. Heat margarine in same saucepan over medium heat until melted. Cook onion and celery in margarine about 3 minutes, stirring occasionally, until crisp-tender. Stir in sage and salt. Mix onion mixture, cherries, stuffing cubes, pecans and broth in large bowl; toss to moisten.

Fill wishbone area of turkey with stuffing. Fasten neck skin to back with skewer. Fold wings across back with tips touching. Fill body cavity lightly with stuffing. (Place any remaining stuffing in small ungreased baking dish; cover and refrigerate. Place in oven with turkey the last 30 minutes of roasting.) Tuck drumsticks under band of skin at tail, or tie or skewer to tail. Place turkey, breast side up, on rack in shallow roasting pan. Brush with margarine. Insert meat thermometer so tip is in thickest part of inside thigh muscle and does not touch bone. Do not add water. Do not cover.

Roast uncovered 3 hours 30 minutes to 4 hours 30 minutes or until thermometer reads 180° and juice of turkey is no longer pink when center of thigh is cut. Place a tent of aluminum foil loosely over turkey when it begins to turn golden. When turkey is two-thirds done, cut band of skin or remove string or skewer holding legs. When turkey is done, remove from oven and let stand about 15 minutes for easier carving. *12 to 14 servings.*

NUTRITION INFORMATION PER SERVING

1 serving		*Percent of U.S. RDA*	
Calories	825	Vitamin A	10%
Protein, g	69	Vitamin C	*
Carbohydrate, g	50	Calcium	12%
Fat, g	39	Iron	34%
Cholesterol, mg	190		
Sodium, mg	750		

Creole Roast Turkey

This flavorful stuffing features many of the same enticing ingredients that are used in the Creole and Cajun cooking of southern Louisiana.

8- to 10-pound turkey

½ cup (1 stick) margarine or butter

1 cup chopped celery (about 2 medium stalks)

½ cup sliced green onions (about 5 medium)

½ cup chopped green bell pepper (about 1 small)

½ teaspoon salt

½ teaspoon ground red pepper (cayenne) or Cajun or Creole seasoning

2 cloves garlic, finely chopped

7 cups dry white bread cubes

1 cup coarsely chopped cooked shrimp (about ½ pound)

1 cup coarsely chopped cooked crabmeat or imitation crabmeat (about 6 ounces)

¼ cup (½ stick) margarine or butter, melted

½ teaspoon Cajun or Creole seasoning

Heat oven to 325°. Prepare turkey as directed on page 9. Heat ½ cup margarine in 1½-quart saucepan over medium heat until melted. Cook celery, green onions, bell pepper, salt, red pepper and garlic in margarine about 3 minutes, stirring occasionally, until vegetables are crisp-tender. Mix vegetable mixture, bread cubes, shrimp and crabmeat in large bowl; toss to moisten.

Fill wishbone area of turkey with stuffing. Fasten neck skin to back with skewer. Fold wings across back with tips touching. Fill body cavity lightly with stuffing. (Place any remaining stuffing in small ungreased baking dish; cover and refrigerate. Place in oven with turkey the last 30 minutes of roasting.) Tuck drumsticks under band of skin at tail, or tie or skewer to tail. Place turkey, breast side up, on rack in shallow roasting pan. Mix ¼ cup margarine and the Cajun seasoning; brush on turkey. Insert meat thermometer so tip is in thickest part of inside thigh muscle and does not touch bone. Do not add water. Do not cover.

Roast uncovered 3 hours 30 minutes to 4 hours 30 minutes or until thermometer reads 180° and juice of turkey is no longer pink when center of thigh is cut. Place a tent of aluminum foil loosely over turkey when it begins to turn golden. When turkey is two-thirds done, cut band of skin or remove string or skewer holding legs. When turkey is done, remove from oven and let stand about 15 minutes for easier carving. *12 to 14 servings.*

NUTRITION INFORMATION PER SERVING

1 serving		Percent of U.S. RDA	
Calories	830	Vitamin A	22%
Protein, g	73	Vitamin C	2%
Carbohydrate, g	45	Calcium	14%
Fat, g	40	Iron	36%
Cholesterol, mg	220		
Sodium, mg	880		

Spice-rubbed Rock Cornish Hens

1 teaspoon ground turmeric

1 teaspoon onion powder

¾ teaspoon garlic powder

½ teaspoon seasoned salt

¼ teaspoon paprika

¼ teaspoon pepper

2 Rock Cornish hens (about 1½ pounds each)

Heat oven to 350°. Mix all ingredients except hens. Rub skins of hens with turmeric mixture. Place hens, breast sides up, on rack in shallow roasting pan. Insert meat thermometer so tip is in thickest part of inside thigh muscle and does not touch bone.

Roast uncovered 1 hour 15 minutes or until thermometer reads 180° and juice of hen is no longer pink when center of thigh is cut. *4 servings.*

TO GRILL: Cut each hen in half along backbone from tail to neck, using poultry shears or kitchen scissors. Rub skins of hens with turmeric mixture. Cover and grill hens, breast sides up, 4 to 6 inches from medium coals 35 minutes; turn hens. Cover and grill 25 to 30 minutes longer or until thermometer reads 180° and juice of hen is no longer pink when center of thigh is cut.

NUTRITION INFORMATION PER SERVING

1 serving		*Percent of U.S. RDA*	
Calories	335	Vitamin A	4%
Protein, g	42	Vitamin C	*
Carbohydrate, g	1	Calcium	4%
Fat, g	18	Iron	14%
Cholesterol, mg	130		
Sodium, mg	380		

Spice-rubbed Rock Cornish Hens

Pieces and Parts

It's so easy to buy chicken in pieces, or to cut up whole chickens. And serving chicken this way makes for easy cooking as well as allowing people to choose their favorite pieces at the table. There are many dishes here that you can pop in the oven and forget until they are done. Try Chinese Barbecued Chicken, Curried Chicken and Broccoli or Indonesian Chicken with Brown Rice. You'll also enjoy skillet dishes such as Tomato-Feta Chicken with Orzo and Elegant Orange-Almond Chicken. There are also grilling instructions where appropriate for those times when you'd like to throw something on the grill. Whatever part you choose, you'll love these recipes!

Elegant Orange-Almond Chicken (page 46)

Chinese Barbecued Chicken

The ingredients found here are used frequently in stir-fry recipes. Experiment with them the next time you stir-fry—they'll add a new level of flavor to whatever you're making.

3 tablespoons hoisin sauce

2 tablespoons apricot preserves

1 tablespoon honey

1½ teaspoons peanut or vegetable oil

1½ teaspoons oyster sauce

1½ teaspoons soy sauce

1½ teaspoons dry sherry

1½ teaspoons finely chopped gingerroot

1 teaspoon chile puree with garlic

¼ teaspoon five-spice powder

1 clove garlic, finely chopped

3- to 3½-pound cut-up broiler-fryer chicken

Heat oven to 325°. Line broiler pan with aluminum foil. Spray rack of broiler pan with nonstick cooking spray. Mix all ingredients except chicken in 1-quart saucepan. Cook over medium-low heat, stirring occasionally, until preserves are melted.

Place chicken, skin sides up, on rack in broiler pan. Brush with preserves mixture. Bake uncovered about 1 hour, brushing occasionally with preserves mixture, until juice of chicken is no longer pink when centers of thickest pieces are cut. Discard any remaining preserves mixture. *6 servings.*

TO GRILL: Place chicken, skin sides up, on grill. Brush with preserves mixture. Cover and grill 4 to 6 inches from medium coals 15 minutes; turn chicken. Brush with preserves mixture. Cover and grill 20 to 40 minutes longer, turning and brushing with preserves mixture, until juice of chicken is no longer pink when centers of thickest pieces are cut. Discard any remaining preserves mixture.

NUTRITION INFORMATION PER SERVING

1 serving		*Percent of U.S. RDA*	
Calories	245	Vitamin A	8%
Protein, g	18	Vitamin C	*
Carbohydrate, g	9	Calcium	2%
Fat, g	15	Iron	6%
Cholesterol, mg	60		
Sodium, mg	530		

Chinese Barbecued Chicken

Oven-fried Chicken

¼ cup (½ stick) margarine or butter

½ cup all-purpose flour

1 teaspoon paprika

½ teaspoon salt

¼ teaspoon pepper

3- to 3½-pound cut-up broiler-fryer chicken

Heat oven to 425°. Heat margarine in rectangular pan, 13×9×2 inches, in oven until melted. Mix flour, paprika, salt and pepper. Coat chicken with flour mixture. Place chicken, skin sides down, in pan. Bake uncovered 30 minutes; turn chicken. Bake uncovered about 30 minutes longer or until juice of chicken is no longer pink when centers of thickest pieces are cut. *6 servings.*

CRUNCHY OVEN-FRIED CHICKEN: Substitute 1 cup cornflake crumbs for the ½ cup flour. Dip chicken into ¼ cup margarine or butter, melted, before coating with crumb mixture.

NUTRITION INFORMATION PER SERVING

1 serving		Percent of U.S. RDA	
Calories	315	Vitamin A	14%
Protein, g	28	Vitamin C	*
Carbohydrate, g	8	Calcium	2%
Fat, g	19	Iron	12%
Cholesterol, mg	85		
Sodium, mg	340		

Oven-barbecued Chicken

3- to 3½-pound cut-up broiler-fryer chicken

¾ cup chile sauce

2 tablespoons honey

1 tablespoon soy sauce

1 teaspoon ground mustard

½ teaspoon prepared horseradish

½ teaspoon red pepper sauce

Heat oven to 375°. Place chicken, skin sides up, in ungreased rectangular pan, 13×9×2 inches. Mix remaining ingredients; pour over chicken. Cover and bake 30 minutes. Spoon sauce in pan over chicken. Bake uncovered about 30 minutes longer or until juice of chicken is no longer pink when centers of thickest pieces are cut. *6 servings.*

NUTRITION INFORMATION PER SERVING

1 serving		Percent of U.S. RDA	
Calories	270	Vitamin A	4%
Protein, g	27	Vitamin C	4%
Carbohydrate, g	14	Calcium	2%
Fat, g	12	Iron	10%
Cholesterol, mg	85		
Sodium, mg	600		

Peppery Horseradish Chicken

3- to 3½-pound cut-up broiler-fryer chicken
¼ cup prepared horseradish
¼ cup sour cream
¼ teaspoon pepper

Heat oven to 325°. Line broiler pan with aluminum foil. Spray rack of broiler pan with nonstick cooking spray. Place chicken, skin sides up, on rack in broiler pan. Mix remaining ingredients; brush on chicken. Bake uncovered about 1 hour 5 minutes, brushing occasionally with horseradish mixture, until juice of chicken is no longer pink when centers of thickest pieces are cut. *6 servings.*

TO GRILL: Place chicken, skin sides up, on grill. Brush with horseradish mixture. Cover and grill 4 to 6 inches from medium coals 15 minutes; turn chicken. Brush with horseradish mixture. Cover and grill 20 to 40 minutes longer, turning and brushing with remaining horseradish mixture, until juice of chicken is no longer pink when centers of thickest pieces are cut.

NUTRITION INFORMATION PER SERVING

1 serving		Percent of U.S. RDA	
Calories	230	Vitamin A	4%
Protein, g	27	Vitamin C	*
Carbohydrate, g	1	Calcium	4%
Fat, g	13	Iron	8%
Cholesterol, mg	90		
Sodium, mg	85		

Zesty Italian Chicken

3- to 3½-pound cut-up broiler-fryer chicken
¼ cup mayonnaise or salad dressing
¼ cup zesty Italian salad dressing
1 teaspoon Italian seasoning

Heat oven to 375°. Place chicken, skin sides down, in ungreased rectangular pan, 13×9×2 inches. Mix remaining ingredients; brush half of mayonnaise mixture on chicken. Cover and bake 30 minutes; turn chicken. Brush with remaining mayonnaise mixture. Bake uncovered about 30 minutes longer or until juice of chicken is no longer pink when centers of thickest pieces are cut. (If chicken begins to brown too quickly, cover with aluminum foil.) *6 servings.*

TO GRILL: Place chicken, skin sides up, on grill. Brush with half of mayonnaise mixture. Cover and grill 5 to 6 inches from medium coals 15 minutes; turn chicken. Cover and grill 20 to 40 minutes longer, turning and brushing with remaining mayonnaise mixture, until juice of chicken is no longer pink when centers of thickest pieces are cut.

NUTRITION INFORMATION PER SERVING

1 serving		Percent of U.S. RDA	
Calories	330	Vitamin A	2%
Protein, g	27	Vitamin C	*
Carbohydrate, g	1	Calcium	2%
Fat, g	24	Iron	10%
Cholesterol, mg	90		
Sodium, mg	240		

Chicken with Tortellini in Cheesy Tomato Sauce

Canned whole tomatoes with added basil, garlic and oregano delicately season this creamy sauce with a mild herb flavor.

1 package (8 ounces) refrigerated cheese-filled tortellini

3- to 3½-pound cut-up broiler-fryer chicken

1½ teaspoons chopped fresh or ½ teaspoon dried basil leaves

¼ teaspoon pepper

2 tablespoons vegetable oil

½ cup chopped onion (about 1 medium)

2 cloves garlic, finely chopped

½ cup ricotta cheese

2 teaspoons sugar

⅛ teaspoon pepper

1 can (14½ ounces) whole tomatoes with basil, garlic and oregano, undrained

Cook tortellini as directed on package; drain. Sprinkle chicken with basil and ¼ teaspoon pepper. Heat oil in 12-inch skillet or Dutch oven over medium heat until hot. Cook chicken in oil about 15 minutes, turning occasionally, until brown on all sides. Cover and cook over low heat about 20 minutes or until juice of chicken is no longer pink when centers of thickest pieces are cut. Remove chicken from skillet, using tongs; keep warm.

Cook onion and garlic in skillet over medium heat about 3 minutes, stirring occasionally, until onion is crisp-tender. Stir in cheese, sugar, ⅛ teaspoon pepper and the tomatoes; break up tomatoes. Heat to boiling; reduce heat. Simmer uncovered about 5 minutes, stirring occasionally, until mixture thickens slightly. Stir in tortellini; heat through. Serve tortellini mixture over chicken. *6 servings.*

NUTRITION INFORMATION PER SERVING

1 serving		*Percent of U.S. RDA*	
Calories	380	Vitamin A	10%
Protein, g	35	Vitamin C	10%
Carbohydrate, g	14	Calcium	14%
Fat, g	21	Iron	16%
Cholesterol, mg	135		
Sodium, mg	370		

Salsa-Chutney Chicken

Chutney, an East Indian relish made with fruit, vinegar, sugar and spices, is combined with salsa for a taste bud–tickling, sweet-hot flavor. Look for chutney among the international ingredients in your grocery store or in specialty food stores.

2 tablespoons vegetable oil

3- to 3½-pound cut-up broiler-fryer chicken

1 clove garlic, finely chopped

¾ cup salsa

¼ cup sliced green onions (2 to 3 medium)

1 jar (9 ounces) chutney (about ¾ cup)

Heat oil in 12-inch skillet or Dutch oven over medium heat until hot. Cook chicken in oil about 15 minutes, turning occasionally, until brown on all sides. Remove chicken from skillet, using tongs.

Drain all but 1 teaspoon drippings from skillet. Cook garlic in 1 teaspoon drippings over medium heat about 15 seconds, stirring constantly, until golden. Stir in remaining ingredients. Place chicken, skin sides up, in skillet. Spoon salsa mixture over chicken. Cover and cook over low heat about 20 minutes, spooning salsa mixture frequently over chicken, until juice of chicken is no longer pink when centers of thickest pieces are cut. *6 servings.*

NUTRITION INFORMATION PER SERVING

1 serving		Percent of U.S. RDA	
Calories	315	Vitamin A	6%
Protein, g	27	Vitamin C	4%
Carbohydrate, g	17	Calcium	2%
Fat, g	16	Iron	10%
Cholesterol, mg	85		
Sodium, mg	410		

Honey-Mustard Chicken

The tangy flavor of mustard seed contrasts delightfully with the sweet honey in this easy-to-prepare recipe.

3- to 3½-pound cut-up broiler-fryer chicken

⅓ cup country-style Dijon mustard

3 tablespoons honey

1 tablespoon mustard seed

½ teaspoon freshly ground pepper

Heat oven to 375°. Place chicken, skin sides down, in ungreased rectangular pan, 13×9×2 inches. Mix remaining ingredients; brush on chicken. Cover and bake 30 minutes; turn chicken. Brush with remaining mustard mixture. Bake uncovered about 30 minutes longer or until juice of chicken is no longer pink when centers of thickest pieces are cut. (If chicken begins to brown too quickly, cover with aluminum foil.) *6 servings.*

TO GRILL: Place chicken, skin sides up, on grill. Brush with mustard mixture. Cover and grill 4 to 6 inches from medium coals 15 minutes; turn chicken. Brush with mustard mixture. Cover and grill 20 to 40 minutes longer, turning and brushing with mustard mixture, until juice of chicken is no longer pink when centers of thickest pieces are cut.

NUTRITION INFORMATION PER SERVING

1 serving		*Percent of U.S. RDA*	
Calories	270	Vitamin A	2%
Protein, g	28	Vitamin C	*
Carbohydrate, g	10	Calcium	4%
Fat, g	13	Iron	10%
Cholesterol, mg	85		
Sodium, mg	240		

Honey-Mustard Chicken

Chicken with Couscous and Black Beans

Couscous, a tiny bead-shaped pasta, is combined with black beans, mandarin oranges and pea pods for a hearty and colorful side dish for chicken in this one-pan recipe.

1 clove garlic, cut in half

3- to 3½-pound cut-up broiler-fryer chicken

¼ teaspoon pepper

2 tablespoons vegetable oil

1 small onion, thinly sliced

2 cloves garlic, finely chopped

3 cups chicken broth

1 can (15 ounces) black beans, rinsed and drained

1 package (10 ounces) couscous

1 can (15 ounces) mandarin orange segments, drained

6 ounces Chinese pea pods (about 2 cups)

Rub cut sides of garlic halves on all sides of chicken; sprinkle with pepper. Heat oil in 12-inch skillet or Dutch oven over medium heat until hot.

Cook chicken in oil about 15 minutes, turning occasionally, until brown on all sides. Cover and cook over low heat about 20 minutes or until juice of chicken is no longer pink when centers of thickest pieces are cut. Remove chicken from skillet, using tongs; keep warm.

Drain all but 1 tablespoon drippings from skillet. Cook onion and chopped garlic in 1 tablespoon drippings over medium heat about 2 minutes, stirring occasionally, until onion is crisp-tender. Stir in broth and beans. Heat to boiling. Stir in remaining ingredients; remove from heat. Cover and let stand about 5 minutes or until couscous is tender and pea pods are hot. Fluff couscous mixture with fork. Serve with chicken. *8 servings.*

NUTRITION INFORMATION PER SERVING

1 serving		Percent of U.S. RDA	
Calories	430	Vitamin A	2%
Protein, g	32	Vitamin C	18%
Carbohydrate, g	52	Calcium	8%
Fat, g	13	Iron	20%
Cholesterol, mg	60		
Sodium, mg	480		

Lemonade-Ginger Chicken

¾ cup water

2 tablespoons finely chopped gingerroot

2 tablespoons vegetable oil

1½ teaspoons fennel seed

½ teaspoon salt

¼ teaspoon pepper

2 cloves garlic, finely chopped

1 can (6-ounce size) frozen lemonade concentrate, thawed

1 tablespoon cornstarch

1 tablespoon water

3- to 3½-pound cut-up broiler-fryer chicken

Mix all ingredients except cornstarch, 1 tablespoon water and the chicken in 1-quart saucepan. Heat to boiling; reduce heat. Simmer uncovered 5 minutes, stirring frequently. Mix cornstarch and 1 tablespoon water; stir into lemonade mixture. Heat to boiling; reduce heat. Simmer uncovered about 1 minute, stirring frequently, until sauce is slightly thickened; remove from heat.

Place chicken in shallow glass or plastic dish. Pour lemonade mixture over chicken. Cover and refrigerate at least 1 hour but no longer than 24 hours, turning occasionally.

Heat oven to 325°. Line broiler pan with aluminum foil. Spray rack of broiler pan with nonstick cooking spray. Remove chicken from marinade; reserve marinade. Place chicken, skin sides up, on rack in broiler pan. Bake uncovered about 1 hour, brushing occasionally with marinade, until juice of chicken is no longer pink when centers of thickest pieces are cut. (If chicken begins to brown too quickly, cover with aluminum foil.) Heat remaining marinade to boiling; boil 1 minute. Serve with chicken. *6 servings.*

TO GRILL: Place marinated chicken, skin sides up, on grill. Brush with marinade. Cover and grill 4 to 6 inches from medium coals 15 minutes; turn chicken. Cover and grill 20 to 40 minutes longer, turning and brushing with marinade, until juice of chicken is no longer pink when centers of thickest pieces are cut. Heat remaining marinade to boiling; boil 1 minute. Serve with chicken.

NUTRITION INFORMATION PER SERVING

1 serving		Percent of U.S. RDA	
Calories	310	Vitamin A	2%
Protein, g	27	Vitamin C	4%
Carbohydrate, g	15	Calcium	2%
Fat, g	16	Iron	10%
Cholesterol, mg	85		
Sodium, mg	260		

Tomato-Feta Chicken with Orzo

Want to peel the pearl onions quickly? Just drop them in boiling water for a few minutes, and the skins will slip right off.

2 tablespoons olive or vegetable oil

3- to 3½-pound cut-up broiler-fryer chicken

1 tablespoon olive or vegetable oil

1¾ cups pearl onions (about 10 ounces)

2 cloves garlic, finely chopped

½ cup white wine or apple juice

2 tablespoons chopped fresh cilantro or parsley

1 tablespoon chopped fresh or 1 teaspoon dried oregano leaves

⅛ teaspoon pepper

2 cans (14½ ounces each) stewed tomatoes, drained

3 cups hot cooked rosamarina (orzo) pasta or rice

2 ounces feta cheese, crumbled

Heat 2 tablespoons oil in 12-inch skillet or Dutch oven over medium heat until hot. Cook chicken in oil about 15 minutes, turning occasionally, until brown on all sides. Remove chicken from skillet, using tongs.

Add 1 tablespoon oil to drippings in skillet. Heat over medium-low heat until hot. Cook onions in oil mixture about 6 minutes, stirring occasionally, until golden brown. Stir in garlic. Cook and stir about 30 seconds or until garlic is light golden brown.

Stir in remaining ingredients except rosamarina and cheese; break up tomatoes. Add chicken. Heat to boiling; reduce heat. Cover and simmer about 20 minutes or until juice of chicken is no longer pink when centers of thickest pieces are cut. Serve tomato mixture over chicken and rosamarina. Sprinkle with cheese and, if desired, additional chopped fresh cilantro. *6 servings.*

NUTRITION INFORMATION PER SERVING

1 serving		Percent of U.S. RDA	
Calories	420	Vitamin A	10%
Protein, g	33	Vitamin C	14%
Carbohydrate, g	28	Calcium	10%
Fat, g	21	Iron	20%
Cholesterol, mg	90		
Sodium, mg	430		

Tomato-Feta Chicken with Orzo

Peanut Butter–Chile Chicken

¾ teaspoon salt

½ teaspoon pepper

3- to 3½-pound cut-up broiler-fryer chicken

2 tablespoons vegetable oil

½ cup chopped onion (about 1 medium)

⅓ cup peanut butter

¼ cup chile sauce

½ teaspoon ground red pepper (cayenne)

1 cup water

¼ cup chopped salted peanuts

¼ cup chopped red bell pepper

Sprinkle salt and pepper over chicken. Heat oil in 12-inch skillet or Dutch oven over medium heat until hot. Cook chicken in oil about 15 minutes, turning occasionally, until brown on all sides. Cover and cook over low heat about 20 minutes or until juice of chicken is no longer pink when centers of thickest pieces are cut. Remove chicken from skillet, using tongs.

Drain all but 1 tablespoon drippings from skillet. Heat 1 tablespoon drippings over medium heat until hot. Cook onion in drippings, stirring occasionally, until tender; reduce heat. Stir in peanut butter, chile sauce and ground red pepper. Gradually stir in water, stirring constantly, until peanut butter is melted. Add chicken. Spoon peanut butter sauce over chicken. Heat to boiling; reduce heat. Simmer uncovered about 5 minutes, spooning sauce frequently over chicken, until sauce is slightly thickened. Serve sauce over chicken. Sprinkle with peanuts and bell pepper. Garnish with chopped fresh basil, if desired. *6 servings.*

NUTRITION INFORMATION PER SERVING

1 serving		Percent of U.S. RDA	
Calories	380	Vitamin A	6%
Protein, g	32	Vitamin C	6%
Carbohydrate, g	6	Calcium	4%
Fat, g	26	Iron	10%
Cholesterol, mg	85		
Sodium, mg	480		

Peanut Butter–Chile Chicken

Crunchy Hazelnut Chicken

To toast the hazelnuts, spread them in an ungreased shallow pan and bake uncovered in a 350° oven 6 to 8 minutes, stirring frequently, until light brown.

1½ cups Sourdough Bread Crumbs (right)

1 package (2¼ ounces) hazelnuts (about ½ cup), toasted

½ cup chopped fresh parsley

½ cup all-purpose flour

¼ teaspoon salt

¼ teaspoon pepper

1 egg or 2 egg whites

3 tablespoons milk

2 tablespoons plain yogurt

2 tablespoons margarine or butter, melted

3- to 3½-pound cut-up broiler-fryer chicken

Prepare Sourdough Bread Crumbs. Increase oven temperature to 375°. Spray rectangular pan, 13×9×2 inches, with nonstick cooking spray.

Place hazelnuts in blender or food processor. Cover and blend, or process, until finely ground. Mix hazelnuts, bread crumbs and parsley.

Mix flour, salt and pepper. Beat egg, milk and yogurt, using fork. Coat chicken with flour mixture. Dip chicken into egg mixture; coat with hazelnut mixture. Place skin sides down in pan. Drizzle with margarine. Bake uncovered 30 minutes; turn chicken. Bake uncovered about 30 minutes longer or until juice of chicken is no longer pink when centers of thickest pieces are cut. *6 servings.*

SOURDOUGH BREAD CRUMBS

Heat oven to 200°. Place 4 or 5 slices sourdough bread, about 7½×½ inch, on rack in oven. Bake about 15 minutes or until bread is dry. Place in blender or food processor. Cover and blend, or process, until fine crumbs form.

NUTRITION INFORMATION PER SERVING

1 serving		*Percent of U.S. RDA*	
Calories	405	Vitamin A	12%
Protein, g	32	Vitamin C	4%
Carbohydrate, g	20	Calcium	8%
Fat, g	23	Iron	18%
Cholesterol, mg	120		
Sodium, mg	330		

Chicken with Lemon-Sage Butter

3- to 3½-pound quartered broiler-fryer chicken

About 10 fresh sage leaves

¼ cup (½ stick) margarine or butter, melted

1 tablespoon chopped fresh or 1 teaspoon dried sage leaves

2 tablespoons lemon juice

1 teaspoon grated lemon peel

⅛ teaspoon salt

⅛ teaspoon pepper

2 cloves garlic, finely chopped

Heat oven to 325°. Spray rack of broiler pan with nonstick cooking spray. Gently loosen skin from each piece of chicken, about halfway back, using fingers. Arrange sage leaves under skin. Pull skin back over chicken. Place chicken, skin sides up and largest pieces to outside, on rack in broiler pan. Mix remaining ingredients; brush on chicken. Bake uncovered about 1 hour 5 minutes or until juice of chicken is no longer pink when centers of thickest pieces are cut. *4 servings.*

NUTRITION INFORMATION PER SERVING

1 serving		*Percent of U.S. RDA*	
Calories	430	Vitamin A	18%
Protein, g	40	Vitamin C	2%
Carbohydrate, g	2	Calcium	6%
Fat, g	29	Iron	14%
Cholesterol, mg	125		
Sodium, mg	320		

Curried Chicken and Broccoli

3- to 3½-pound cut-up broiler-fryer chicken

½ cup sour cream

½ cup orange juice

1 tablespoon chopped fresh or 1 teaspoon dried basil leaves

1 tablespoon chopped fresh or 1 teaspoon dried oregano leaves

1 teaspoon curry powder

⅛ teaspoon chile powder

⅛ teaspoon ground cinnamon

1 can (10¾ ounces) condensed cream of chicken soup

1 package (16 ounces) frozen broccoli cuts, thawed and drained

Heat oven to 375°. Place chicken, skin sides up, in ungreased rectangular pan, 13×9×2 inches. Bake uncovered about 50 minutes or until chicken is golden brown. Remove excess fat from pan.

Mix remaining ingredients except broccoli; spoon over and around chicken. Arrange broccoli around chicken. Cover tightly and bake about 50 minutes or until juice of chicken is no longer pink when centers of thickest pieces are cut and broccoli is crisp-tender. *6 servings.*

NUTRITION INFORMATION PER SERVING

1 serving		*Percent of U.S. RDA*	
Calories	320	Vitamin A	22%
Protein, g	31	Vitamin C	30%
Carbohydrate, g	11	Calcium	10%
Fat, g	18	Iron	14%
Cholesterol, mg	100		
Sodium, mg	500		

Chicken with Pineapple-Pecan Stuffing

*1½ teaspoons chopped fresh or ½
teaspoon dried thyme leaves*

¼ teaspoon salt

⅛ teaspoon pepper

*3- to 3½-pound cut-up broiler-fryer
chicken*

2 tablespoons vegetable oil

1 cup chopped onion (about 1 large)

½ cup shredded carrot (about 1 small)

3 cups herb-seasoned cubed stuffing mix

¾ cup chopped pecans, toasted if desired

½ cup chopped fresh parsley

*1 can (8 ounces) pineapple tidbits in juice,
drained and juice reserved*

¼ cup chicken broth

Mix thyme, salt and pepper; sprinkle over chicken. Heat oil in 12-inch skillet or Dutch oven over medium heat until hot. Cook chicken in oil about 15 minutes, turning occasionally, until brown on all sides. Remove chicken from skillet, using tongs; drain on paper towels. Drain all but 1 tablespoon drippings from skillet.

Heat oven to 375°. Grease rectangular pan, 13×9×2 inches. Heat 1 tablespoon drippings in skillet over medium heat until hot. Cook onion in drippings, stirring frequently, until tender; remove from heat. Stir in carrot, stuffing mix, pecans and parsley. Stir in pineapple. Drizzle reserved pineapple juice and the broth over stuffing; toss. Spoon stuffing into pan. Place chicken, skin sides up, on stuffing. Cover tightly and bake about 50 minutes or until juice of chicken is no longer pink when centers of thickest pieces are cut. Fluff stuffing with fork. Serve with chicken. *6 servings.*

NUTRITION INFORMATION PER SERVING

1 serving		Percent of U.S. RDA	
Calories	565	Vitamin A	24%
Protein, g	35	Vitamin C	10%
Carbohydrate, g	48	Calcium	10%
Fat, g	28	Iron	26%
Cholesterol, mg	85		
Sodium, mg	570		

Chicken with Pineapple-Pecan Stuffing

Sun-dried Tomato and Apricot Chicken

If you prefer to use sun-dried tomatoes that aren't packed in oil, pour enough hot water over the dried tomatoes to cover them. Let them stand 10 to 15 minutes to soften; drain. You'll need 1½ cups of the softened tomatoes.

½ cup orange juice

2 tablespoons balsamic vinegar

3- to 3½-pound cut-up broiler-fryer chicken

½ teaspoon salt

¼ teaspoon pepper

⅓ cup orange marmalade

1 jar (8 ounces) sun-dried tomatoes in oil, drained

1 package (6 ounces) dried apricots

3 tablespoons packed brown sugar

Heat oven to 375°. Mix orange juice and vinegar in ungreased rectangular pan, 13×9×2 inches. Arrange chicken, skin sides up, in pan. Spoon orange juice mixture over chicken. Sprinkle with salt and pepper. Spread marmalade over chicken. Bake uncovered 30 minutes.

Spoon orange juice mixture over chicken. Sprinkle tomatoes and apricots around chicken; toss with orange juice mixture. Sprinkle brown sugar over tomatoes and apricots. Bake uncovered 35 to 40 minutes, spooning orange juice mixture frequently over chicken, until juice of chicken is no longer pink when centers of thickest pieces are cut. (Cover pan loosely with aluminum foil when chicken begins to brown.) *6 servings.*

NUTRITION INFORMATION PER SERVING

1 serving		Percent of U.S. RDA	
Calories	375	Vitamin A	26%
Protein, g	29	Vitamin C	18%
Carbohydrate, g	41	Calcium	4%
Fat, g	12	Iron	18%
Cholesterol, mg	85		
Sodium, mg	270		

Cuban Glazed Chicken

2 tablespoons lime juice

1 tablespoon olive or vegetable oil

1 teaspoon ground cumin

½ teaspoon salt

⅛ teaspoon pepper

2 cloves garlic, finely chopped

3- to 3½-pound cut-up broiler-fryer chicken

¼ cup guava or apple jelly

¼ cup guava fruit drink or apple juice

2 tablespoons lime juice

½ teaspoon Worcestershire sauce

½ teaspoon cider vinegar

¼ teaspoon paprika

⅛ teaspoon ground cumin

1 jalapeño chile, seeded and finely chopped

Mix 2 tablespoons lime juice, the oil, 1 teaspoon cumin, the salt, pepper and garlic in sealable heavy-duty plastic bag. Add chicken; seal bag and turn to coat with marinade. Refrigerate at least 1 hour but no longer than 24 hours, turning bag occasionally.

Heat oven to 325°. Line broiler pan with aluminum foil. Spray rack of broiler pan with nonstick cooking spray. Remove chicken from marinade; discard marinade. Place chicken, skin sides up, on rack in broiler pan. Bake uncovered 30 minutes.

Heat remaining ingredients to boiling in 1-quart saucepan; reduce heat. Simmer uncovered about 5 minutes, stirring frequently, until mixture thickens and is reduced by about half; remove from heat. Brush chicken with jelly mixture. Bake uncovered about 30 minutes longer, brushing frequently with jelly mixture, until juice of chicken is no longer pink when centers of thickest pieces are cut. *6 servings.*

TO GRILL: Cover and grill marinated chicken, skin sides up, 5 to 6 inches from medium coals 15 minutes; turn chicken. Brush with jelly mixture. Cover and grill 20 to 40 minutes longer, turning and brushing frequently with jelly mixture, until juice of chicken is no longer pink when centers of thickest pieces are cut. Discard any unused jelly mixture.

NUTRITION INFORMATION PER SERVING

1 serving		*Percent of U.S. RDA*	
Calories	260	Vitamin A	10%
Protein, g	27	Vitamin C	14%
Carbohydrate, g	11	Calcium	2%
Fat, g	12	Iron	10%
Cholesterol, mg	85		
Sodium, mg	130		

Elegant Orange-Almond Chicken

You can add a touch of the Orient to this fancy, yet easy, recipe by using a combination of button, shiitake and enoki mushrooms.

½ cup all-purpose flour

½ teaspoon salt

¼ teaspoon pepper

3- to 3½-pound cut-up broiler-fryer chicken

2 tablespoons vegetable oil

3 cups sliced mushrooms (about 8 ounces)

¼ cup orange juice

¼ cup almond-flavored liqueur or orange juice

2 tablespoons sliced almonds

2 tablespoons chopped fresh cilantro or parsley

Mix flour, salt and pepper. Coat chicken with flour mixture. Heat oil in 12-inch skillet or Dutch oven over medium heat until hot. Cook chicken in oil about 15 minutes, turning occasionally, until brown on all sides. Cover and cook over low heat about 20 minutes or until juice of chicken is no longer pink when centers of thickest pieces are cut. Remove chicken from skillet, using tongs; keep warm.

Drain all but 1 tablespoon drippings from skillet. Cook mushrooms in 1 tablespoon drippings over medium heat about 2 minutes, stirring occasionally, until tender. Remove mushrooms from skillet. Heat skillet over medium-high heat. Add orange juice and liqueur. Cook 1 to 2 minutes, stirring constantly and scraping up any brown bits, until mixture is slightly thickened. Stir in mushrooms; heat through. Serve mushroom mixture over chicken. Sprinkle with almonds and cilantro. *6 servings.*

NUTRITION INFORMATION PER SERVING

1 serving		Percent of U.S. RDA	
Calories	335	Vitamin A	2%
Protein, g	29	Vitamin C	6%
Carbohydrate, g	15	Calcium	2%
Fat, g	18	Iron	14%
Cholesterol, mg	85		
Sodium, mg	250		

Chicken with Apple–Sour Cream Sauce

Spinach fettuccine makes a lovely backdrop for the silky-white sour cream sauce with red apple slices. For the fastest-cooking fettuccine, buy the fresh variety, located in the refrigerated section of your supermarket.

1 tablespoon chopped fresh or 1 teaspoon crumbled dried sage leaves

⅛ teaspoon pepper

3- to 3½-pound cut-up broiler-fryer chicken

3 tablespoons vegetable oil

1 medium unpeeled all-purpose red apple, thinly sliced

¼ cup chopped onion (about 1 small)

¾ teaspoon chopped fresh or ¼ teaspoon crumbled dried sage leaves

¼ teaspoon salt

2 tablespoons all-purpose flour

⅔ cup sour cream

⅓ cup plain yogurt

About 3 tablespoons milk

3 cups hot cooked spinach fettuccine

Chopped fresh chives, if desired

Mix 1 tablespoon sage and the pepper; sprinkle over chicken. Heat oil in 12-inch skillet or Dutch oven over medium heat until hot. Cook chicken in oil about 15 minutes, turning occasionally, until brown on all sides. Cover and cook over low heat about 20 minutes or until juice of chicken is no longer pink when centers of thickest pieces are cut. Remove chicken from skillet, using tongs; keep warm.

Drain all but 1 tablespoon drippings from skillet. Cook apple, onion, ¾ teaspoon sage and the salt in 1 tablespoon drippings over medium heat about 2 minutes, stirring occasionally, until onion is crisp-tender. Stir in flour. Cook over medium heat, stirring constantly, until mixture is smooth and bubbly; remove from heat. Stir in sour cream and yogurt. Cook over medium heat, stirring constantly, until mixture is thickened and bubbly. Cook and stir 1 minute longer. Stir in milk, 1 tablespoon at a time, until mixture is creamy. Serve sauce over chicken and fettuccine. Sprinkle with chives. *6 servings.*

NUTRITION INFORMATION PER SERVING

1 serving		Percent of U.S. RDA	
Calories	460	Vitamin A	6%
Protein, g	33	Vitamin C	2%
Carbohydrate, g	28	Calcium	8%
Fat, g	25	Iron	16%
Cholesterol, mg	130		
Sodium, mg	320		

Yogurt-Lime–marinated Chicken

3- to 3½-pound cut-up broiler-fryer chicken

¼ teaspoon salt

⅛ teaspoon pepper

¾ cup plain low-fat yogurt

1 tablespoon vegetable oil

1 tablespoon lime juice

1 teaspoon honey

1 teaspoon finely chopped gingerroot

1 clove garlic, finely chopped

1 medium lime, thinly sliced

Place chicken in shallow glass or plastic dish. Sprinkle with salt and pepper. Mix remaining ingredients except lime slices; pour evenly over chicken. Cover and refrigerate at least 1 hour but no longer than 24 hours, turning occasionally.

Heat oven to 375°. Remove chicken from marinade; discard marinade. Arrange chicken, skin sides up, in ungreased rectangular pan, 13×9×2 inches. Arrange lime slices on chicken. Cover and bake 20 minutes. Remove lime slices; discard. Bake uncovered about 40 minutes longer or until juice of chicken is no longer pink when centers of thickest pieces are cut. Garnish with additional lime slices if desired. *6 servings.*

TO GRILL: Cut lime in half instead of into slices. Place marinated chicken, skin sides up, on grill. Squeeze juice from lime halves over chicken. Cover and grill 5 to 6 inches from medium coals 15 minutes; turn chicken. Cover and grill 20 to 40 minutes longer, turning occasionally, until juice of chicken is no longer pink when centers of thickest pieces are cut.

NUTRITION INFORMATION PER SERVING

1 serving		*Percent of U.S. RDA*	
Calories	220	Vitamin A	2%
Protein, g	27	Vitamin C	*
Carbohydrate, g	1	Calcium	4%
Fat, g	12	Iron	8%
Cholesterol, mg	85		
Sodium, mg	130		

Margarita Chicken

Serve up some corn bread spiked with jalapeño chiles and shredded Cheddar cheese for a spicy accompaniment to this south-of-the-border chicken.

½ cup nonalcoholic margarita mix

3 tablespoons lime juice

1 clove garlic, crushed

3- to 3½-pound cut-up broiler-fryer chicken

1 teaspoon coarse salt

Mix margarita mix, lime juice and garlic in sealable heavy-duty plastic bag. Add chicken; seal bag and turn to coat with marinade. Refrigerate at least 1 hour but no longer than 24 hours, turning bag occasionally. Remove chicken from marinade; reserve marinade.

Heat oven to 375°. Line broiler pan with aluminum foil. Spray rack of broiler pan with nonstick cooking spray. Place chicken, skin sides down, on rack in broiler pan. Brush with marinade; sprinkle with ½ teaspoon of the salt. Bake uncovered 30 minutes; turn chicken. Brush with remaining marinade; sprinkle with remaining ½ teaspoon salt. Bake uncovered about 35 minutes longer or until juice of chicken is no longer pink when centers of thickest pieces are cut. (If chicken begins to brown too quickly, cover with aluminum foil.) *6 servings.*

TO GRILL: Place marinated chicken, skin sides up, on grill. Brush with marinade; sprinkle with ½ teaspoon of the salt. Cover and grill 5 to 6 inches from medium coals 15 minutes; turn chicken. Brush with remaining marinade; sprinkle with remaining ½ teaspoon salt. Cover and grill 20 to 40 minutes longer, turning occasionally, until juice of chicken is no longer pink when centers of thickest pieces are cut.

NUTRITION INFORMATION PER SERVING

1 serving		*Percent of U.S. RDA*	
Calories	230	Vitamin A	2%
Protein, g	27	Vitamin C	6%
Carbohydrate, g	3	Calcium	2%
Fat, g	12	Iron	8%
Cholesterol, mg	85		
Sodium, mg	340		

Hot-and-Sour Chicken

2 tablespoons vegetable oil

3- to 3½-pound cut-up broiler-fryer chicken

1 cup water

1 tablespoon plus 1 teaspoon sugar

3 tablespoons soy sauce

2 tablespoons rice vinegar

1½ teaspoons Worcestershire sauce

½ teaspoon sesame oil

¼ teaspoon pepper

1 tablespoon finely chopped gingerroot

2 cloves garlic, finely chopped

¼ cup sliced green onions (2 to 3 medium)

2 teaspoons chile puree with garlic

2 tablespoons cornstarch

2 tablespoons cold water

Heat vegetable oil in 12-inch skillet or Dutch oven over medium heat until hot. Cook chicken in oil about 15 minutes, turning occasionally, until brown on all sides. Remove chicken from skillet, using tongs. Drain all but 1 tablespoon drippings from skillet. Mix 1 cup water, the sugar, soy sauce, vinegar, Worcestershire sauce, sesame oil and pepper; reserve.

Heat 1 tablespoon drippings in skillet over medium heat. Cook and stir gingerroot, garlic, green onions and chile puree in drippings 15 seconds. Stir in soy sauce mixture. Add chicken. Heat to boiling; reduce heat. Cover and simmer about 20 minutes, turning chicken after 10 minutes, until juice of chicken is no longer pink when centers of thickest pieces are cut.

Remove chicken from skillet to serving platter, using tongs; keep warm. Mix cornstarch and 2 tablespoons cold water. Heat mixture in skillet to boiling; stir in cornstarch mixture. Boil and stir 1 minute. Spoon over chicken. *6 servings.*

NUTRITION INFORMATION PER SERVING

1 serving		Percent of U.S. RDA	
Calories	295	Vitamin A	2%
Protein, g	27	Vitamin C	2%
Carbohydrate, g	8	Calcium	2%
Fat, g	17	Iron	10%
Cholesterol, mg	85		
Sodium, mg	610		

Indonesian Chicken with Brown Rice

3- to 3½-pound cut-up broiler-fryer
chicken

2 tablespoons margarine or butter, melted

1 cup uncooked quick-cooking brown rice

½ cup chopped onion (about 1 medium)

⅓ cup chopped fresh parsley

1½ cups boiling water

½ cup orange juice

⅓ cup tomato sauce

2 tablespoons packed brown sugar

3 tablespoons soy sauce

2 tablespoons white wine vinegar

1 teaspoon ground cinnamon

½ teaspoon ground nutmeg

⅛ teaspoon ground cloves

Heat oven to 425°. Place chicken, skin sides up, in ungreased rectangular pan, 13×9×2 inches. Brush with margarine. Bake uncovered about 30 minutes or until golden brown. Remove chicken from pan; drain fat from pan.

Reduce oven temperature to 375°. Mix remaining ingredients; pour into pan. Place chicken, skin sides up, in rice mixture. Cover tightly and bake about 40 minutes or until juice of chicken is no longer pink when centers of thickest pieces are cut and liquid in pan is absorbed. Fluff rice mixture with fork. Serve with chicken. *6 servings.*

NUTRITION INFORMATION PER SERVING

1 serving		Percent of U.S. RDA	
Calories	390	Vitamin A	10%
Protein, g	30	Vitamin C	12%
Carbohydrate, g	34	Calcium	4%
Fat, g	16	Iron	14%
Cholesterol, mg	85		
Sodium, mg	720		

Chinese Pepper Chicken

2 tablespoons soy sauce

2 tablespoons rice wine vinegar

1 teaspoon sugar

2 teaspoons sesame oil

½ teaspoon red pepper sauce

3- to 3½-pound cut-up broiler-fryer chicken

2 tablespoons vegetable oil

1 teaspoon finely chopped gingerroot

2 cloves garlic, finely chopped

¼ cup sliced green onions (2 to 3 medium)

1½ cups sliced mushrooms

3 medium bell peppers, cut into 1-inch pieces

Mix soy sauce, vinegar, sugar, sesame oil and pepper sauce in sealable heavy-duty plastic bag. Add chicken; seal bag and turn to coat with marinade. Refrigerate at least 1 hour but no longer than 24 hours, turning bag occasionally. Remove chicken from marinade; reserve marinade.

Heat vegetable oil in 12-inch skillet or Dutch oven over medium heat until hot. Cook chicken in oil about 15 minutes, turning occasionally, until brown on all sides. Cover and cook over low heat about 20 minutes or until juice of chicken is no longer pink when centers of thickest pieces are cut. Remove chicken from skillet, using tongs; keep warm.

Drain all but 1 teaspoon drippings from skillet. Heat 1 teaspoon drippings and the marinade in skillet over medium-high heat. Stir in gingerroot, garlic and green onions. Cook and stir about 30 seconds or until garlic is light golden brown. Stir in mushrooms and bell peppers. Cook about 5 minutes, stirring occasionally, until bell peppers are crisp-tender. Serve with chicken. *6 servings.*

NUTRITION INFORMATION PER SERVING

1 serving		Percent of U.S. RDA	
Calories	295	Vitamin A	4%
Protein, g	28	Vitamin C	30%
Carbohydrate, g	6	Calcium	4%
Fat, g	18	Iron	12%
Cholesterol, mg	85		
Sodium, mg	420		

Chinese Pepper Chicken

Baked Chicken with Gremolada

3- to 3½-pound cut-up broiler-fryer chicken
1 tablespoon olive or vegetable oil
1 tablespoon lemon juice
½ teaspoon salt
⅛ teaspoon pepper
2 cloves garlic, finely chopped
Gremolada (right)

Heat oven to 375°. Place chicken, skin sides up, in ungreased rectangular pan, 13×9×2 inches. Mix oil, lemon juice, salt, pepper and garlic; brush on chicken. Cover and bake 30 minutes. Bake uncovered about 40 minutes longer or until juice of chicken is no longer pink when centers of thickest pieces are cut. Serve with Gremolada. *6 servings.*

GREMOLADA

½ cup chopped fresh parsley
1 tablespoon grated lemon peel
Dash of salt
Dash of pepper
2 cloves garlic, crushed

Mix all ingredients.

TO GRILL: Brush chicken with oil mixture. Cover and grill chicken, skin sides up, 4 to 6 inches from medium coals 15 minutes; turn chicken. Cover and grill 20 to 40 minutes longer, turning occasionally, until juice of chicken is no longer pink when centers of thickest pieces are cut.

NUTRITION INFORMATION PER SERVING

1 serving		Percent of U.S. RDA	
Calories	240	Vitamin A	4%
Protein, g	27	Vitamin C	6%
Carbohydrate, g	1	Calcium	2%
Fat, g	14	Iron	10%
Cholesterol, mg	85		
Sodium, mg	300		

Baked Chicken with Gremolada

Baked Chicken with Cranberry-Tomato Chutney

The tomato skins will slip off easily if you dip tomatoes in boiling water for about 30 seconds.

Cranberry-Tomato Chutney (right)

3- to 3½-pound cut-up broiler-fryer chicken

Reserved whole berry cranberry sauce (from chutney recipe)

⅛ teaspoon pepper

Prepare Cranberry-Tomato Chutney. Heat oven to 375°. Place chicken, skin sides down, in ungreased rectangular pan, 13×9×2 inches. Heat reserved cranberry sauce and the pepper in 1-quart saucepan over low heat, stirring constantly, until spreading consistency; remove from heat. Brush on chicken. Cover and bake 30 minutes; turn chicken. Brush with remaining cranberry sauce mixture (reheat if necessary). Bake uncovered about 40 minutes longer or until juice of chicken is no longer pink when centers of thickest pieces are cut. Serve with chutney. *6 servings.*

CRANBERRY-TOMATO CHUTNEY

1 can (16 ounces) whole berry cranberry sauce

½ cup raisins

2 tablespoons sugar

1 teaspoon finely chopped gingerroot

½ teaspoon salt

2 large tomatoes, peeled, seeded and coarsely chopped (about 1½ cups)

Reserve half of cranberry sauce to brush on chicken. Mix remaining cranberry sauce and remaining ingredients in 2-quart saucepan. Heat to boiling; reduce heat. Simmer uncovered about 15 minutes or until thickened. Cool slightly. Cover and refrigerate about 2 hours or until chilled.

TO GRILL: Cover and grill chicken, skin sides up, 4 to 6 inches from medium coals 15 minutes; turn chicken. Brush with cranberry sauce mixture. Cover and grill 20 to 40 minutes longer, turning and brushing with remaining cranberry sauce mixture, until juice of chicken is no longer pink when centers of thickest pieces are cut.

NUTRITION INFORMATION PER SERVING

1 serving		Percent of U.S. RDA	
Calories	400	Vitamin A	6%
Protein, g	28	Vitamin C	10%
Carbohydrate, g	47	Calcium	2%
Fat, g	12	Iron	12%
Cholesterol, mg	85		
Sodium, mg	280		

Chicken and Prosciutto with Lentils

Prosciutto is a lean, salt-cured Italian ham that is traditionally aged for one year. It has a tender texture with minimal salt flavor.

1 tablespoon margarine or butter

1 tablespoon vegetable oil

3- to 3½-pound cut-up broiler-fryer chicken

1 cup dried lentils, sorted and rinsed

½ cup ½-inch pieces prosciutto or Canadian-style bacon (about 3 ounces)

½ cup shredded carrot (about 1 small)

¼ cup chopped fresh parsley

⅛ teaspoon pepper

1 medium onion, thinly sliced and separated into rings

1 clove garlic, finely chopped

1½ cups chicken broth

½ cup ketchup

1 teaspoon ground mustard

Heat margarine and oil in 12-inch skillet or Dutch oven over medium heat until hot. Cook chicken in margarine mixture about 15 minutes, turning occasionally, until brown on all sides; drain.

Heat oven to 400°. Grease rectangular pan, 13×9×2 inches. Mix lentils, prosciutto, carrot, parsley, pepper, onion and garlic in pan. Mix remaining ingredients; pour over lentil mixture. Place chicken, skin sides up, on lentil mixture. Cover tightly and bake about 50 minutes or until juice of chicken is no longer pink when centers of thickest pieces are cut and lentils are tender. *6 servings.*

NUTRITION INFORMATION PER SERVING

1 serving		Percent of U.S. RDA	
Calories	410	Vitamin A	26%
Protein, g	40	Vitamin C	10%
Carbohydrate, g	28	Calcium	6%
Fat, g	18	Iron	28%
Cholesterol, mg	90		
Sodium, mg	710		

Grilling Know-how

Just about everyone loves to grill, whether it's in the backyard, at a picnic site, on a balcony hibachi or on a stovetop grill. Food cooked over an open flame just always seems to taste better! Grilling is a simple pleasure, but you do need to do a little homework, then take a few trial runs to build confidence. The following information and chart will help you get started.

Lighting Coals

- Light coals at least 30 minutes before cooking begins to ensure proper temperature is reached. Most coals take between 30 to 45 minutes to reach proper temperature.

- When are the coals ready? In the daylight, the coals should be completely covered with light gray ash. After dark, the coals will glow red.

Direct Heat: In this method, poultry is cooked directly over the heat. This method is used in all recipes in this book except for whole chicken, whole turkey and whole turkey breast.

Indirect Method: This is the preferred method for longer cooking poultry such as whole birds and whole turkey breasts. In this method, poultry is cooked away from the heat. When using coals, arrange around edge of firebox and place drip pan under grilling area. If using a dual-burner gas grill, heat only one side and place food under the burner that is not lit. For single-burner gas grills, place food in foil tray or on several layers of aluminum foil and use **low** heat (cooking times may be longer than chart indicates).

Grill Rack

- Grease or oil the rack before coals are lighted or the gas is turned on.

- Place the grill rack 4 to 6 inches above the coals or gas burners.

Cooking

- For even cooking, place meatier poultry pieces in the center of the grill rack and smaller pieces on the edges and turn pieces frequently.

- To retain poultry juices, turn pieces with tongs instead of a fork.

- To prevent overbrowning or burning, brush sauces on during the last 15 to 20 minutes of cooking, especially those containing tomato or sugar.

FOOD SAFETY

- Never serve cooked poultry on the same un-washed platter on which raw poultry was carried to the grill.

- Marinades and sauces left over from contact with raw poultry must be heated to boiling and boiled 1 minute before being served.

GRILLING POULTRY

Type of Poultry	Weight (pounds)	Grilling Method	Temperature	Cooking Time and Doneness
Whole chicken	3 to 3½	Indirect heat	Medium	1 to 1½ hours or until meat thermometer reads 180°F and juice of chicken is no longer pink when center of thigh is cut.
Whole turkey	8 to 10	Indirect heat	Medium	3 to 4 hours or until meat thermometer reads 180°F and juice of turkey is no longer pink when center of thigh is cut.
Whole turkey breast	3½ to 4	Indirect heat	Medium	1 to 1¼ hours or until meat thermometer reads 170°F and juice of turkey is no longer pink when center is cut.
Rock Cornish hen	3 (split birds in half before grilling for best results)	Direct heat	Medium	30 to 40 minutes or until meat thermometer reads 180°F and juice of hen is no longer pink when center of thigh is cut.
Cut-up chicken	3 to 3½	Direct heat	Medium	35 to 40 minutes or until juice of chicken is no longer pink when centers of thickest pieces are cut. **Note:** Dark meat may take longer to cook.
Chicken breasts (with bone)	1	Direct	Medium	20 to 25 minutes or until juice of chicken is no longer pink when centers of thickest pieces are cut.

(Recipes continue on following page)

GRILLING POULTRY (*continued*)

Type of Poultry	Weight (pounds)	Grilling Method	Temperature	Cooking Time and Doneness
Chicken breasts (boneless and not flattened)	1	Direct	Medium	15 to 20 minutes or until juice of chicken is no longer pink when centers of thickest pieces are cut.
Chicken breasts (boneless and flattened to ¼-inch thickness)	1	Direct	Medium	10 to 15 minutes or until juice of chicken is no longer pink when centers of thickest pieces are cut.
Chicken wings	2 to 2½	Direct	Medium	12 to 18 minutes or until juice of chicken is no longer pink when centers of thickest pieces are cut.
Ground chicken or turkey patties	1 (½-inch thick patties)	Direct	Medium	15 to 20 minutes or until no longer pink.
Turkey tenderloins	1 to 1½	Direct	Medium	20 to 30 minutes or until juice of turkey is no longer pink when centers of thickest pieces are cut.
Turkey breast slices	1 to 1½	Direct	Medium	8 to 10 minutes or until juice of turkey is no longer pink when centers of thickest pieces are cut.

Chicken and Sausage Cassoulet

½ pound bulk mild Italian sausage

1 tablespoon vegetable oil

3- to 3½-pound cut-up broiler-fryer chicken

½ cup chopped onion (about 1 medium)

1 cup water

½ cup dry red wine or tomato juice

1½ teaspoons chopped fresh or ½ teaspoon dried thyme leaves

⅛ teaspoon ground cloves

3 medium carrots, cut into ½-inch pieces

2 cloves garlic, finely chopped

2 bay leaves

1 can (6 ounces) tomato paste

1 can (15 to 16 ounces) navy beans, drained

1 can (15 to 16 ounces) pinto beans, drained

Cook sausage in Dutch oven over medium heat, stirring occasionally, until brown. Remove sausage from Dutch oven, using slotted spoon; drain on paper towels. (Do not drain drippings from Dutch oven.) Heat sausage drippings and oil in Dutch oven over medium heat until hot. Cook chicken in drippings mixture about 15 minutes, turning occasionally, until brown on all sides. Remove chicken from Dutch oven, using tongs.

Mix sausage and remaining ingredients in Dutch oven. Add chicken. Heat to boiling; reduce heat. Cover and simmer 30 minutes. Uncover and simmer about 10 minutes longer or until juice of chicken is no longer pink when centers of thickest pieces are cut and carrots are tender. Discard bay leaves. *8 servings.*

NUTRITION INFORMATION PER SERVING

1 serving		Percent of U.S. RDA	
Calories	500	Vitamin A	68%
Protein, g	46	Vitamin C	10%
Carbohydrate, g	37	Calcium	12%
Fat, g	23	Iron	32%
Cholesterol, mg	115		
Sodium, mg	790		

Robust Chicken Stew

¼ pound bacon, cut into 1-inch pieces

3 medium onions, thinly sliced

1 cup thinly sliced carrots (about 2 medium)

1 cup chopped bell pepper (about 1 medium)

2 cups beer or nonalcoholic beer

2 cups chicken broth

1 tablespoon chopped fresh or 1 teaspoon dried thyme leaves

½ teaspoon pepper

3- to 3½-pound cut-up broiler-fryer chicken

6 ounces uncooked dumpling egg noodles (about 3 cups)

½ cup cold water

¼ cup all-purpose flour

Cook bacon in Dutch oven over medium heat, stirring frequently, until crisp. Remove bacon from Dutch oven, using slotted spoon; drain on paper towels. (Do not drain bacon fat from Dutch oven.) Cook onions in bacon fat over medium heat about 4 minutes, stirring frequently, until crisp-tender.

Stir in bacon, carrots, bell pepper, beer, broth, thyme and pepper. Add chicken. Heat to boiling; reduce heat. Cover and simmer 25 minutes. Heat to boiling; stir in noodles. Boil uncovered about 12 minutes or until juice of chicken is no longer pink when centers of thickest pieces are cut and noodles are tender. Shake water and flour in tightly covered container; gradually stir into stew. Heat to boiling; boil and stir 1 minute. *6 servings.*

NUTRITION INFORMATION PER SERVING

1 serving		Percent of U.S. RDA	
Calories	410	Vitamin A	84%
Protein, g	35	Vitamin C	16%
Carbohydrate, g	35	Calcium	6%
Fat, g	16	Iron	22%
Cholesterol, mg	110		
Sodium, mg	450		

Golden Parmesan Chicken

1¼ cups grated Parmesan cheese

¼ teaspoon pepper

3- to 3½-pound cut-up broiler-fryer chicken

⅓ cup margarine or butter, melted

Heat oven to 425°. Mix cheese and pepper. Brush chicken with margarine; coat with cheese mixture. Place skin sides down in ungreased rectangular pan, 13×9×2 inches. Pour any remaining margarine over chicken.

Bake uncovered 30 minutes; turn chicken. Bake about 20 minutes longer or until juice is no longer pink when centers of thickest pieces are cut. *4 servings.*

NUTRITION INFORMATION PER SERVING

1 serving		Percent of U.S. RDA	
Calories	565	Vitamin A	26%
Protein, g	51	Vitamin C	*
Carbohydrate, g	1	Calcium	38%
Fat, g	40	Iron	14%
Cholesterol, mg	140		
Sodium, mg	750		

Chicken with Honey-caramelized Onions

3- to 3½-pound cut-up broiler-fryer chicken

⅛ teaspoon pepper

1 tablespoon margarine or butter

1 tablespoon vegetable oil

1 tablespoon honey

2 tablespoons margarine or butter

3 large onions, thinly sliced

2 tablespoons honey

1 teaspoon ground mustard

¼ cup sweet white wine or nonalcoholic wine

Sprinkle chicken with pepper. Heat 1 tablespoon margarine and the oil in 12-inch skillet or Dutch oven over medium heat until hot. Cook chicken in margarine mixture about 15 minutes, turning occasionally, until brown on all sides. Cover and cook over low heat about 20 minutes or until juice of chicken is no longer pink when centers of thickest pieces are cut. Remove chicken from skillet. Brush with 1 tablespoon honey; keep warm. Drain drippings from skillet.

Heat 2 tablespoons margarine in skillet until melted. Cook onions in margarine over medium-high heat about 8 minutes, stirring frequently, until transparent. Stir in 2 tablespoons honey. Cook about 3 minutes, stirring frequently, until onions are caramel colored. Mix mustard and wine; pour over onions. Cook over medium heat about 2 minutes, stirring frequently, until liquid is absorbed. Serve onions with chicken. *6 servings.*

TO GRILL: Sprinkle chicken with pepper. Mix 1 tablespoon margarine or butter, melted, and the oil. Place chicken, skin sides up, on grill. Brush with margarine mixture. Cover and grill 4 to 6 inches from medium coals 15 minutes; turn chicken. Brush with margarine mixture. Cover and grill 20 to 40 minutes longer, turning occasionally, until juice of chicken is no longer pink when centers of thickest pieces are cut. Brush with 1 tablespoon honey; keep warm while preparing onions.

NUTRITION INFORMATION PER SERVING

1 serving		Percent of U.S. RDA	
Calories	345	Vitamin A	10%
Protein, g	28	Vitamin C	4%
Carbohydrate, g	15	Calcium	4%
Fat, g	20	Iron	10%
Cholesterol, mg	85		
Sodium, mg	140		

Zesty Roasted Chicken and Potatoes

3- to 3½-pound cut-up broiler-fryer chicken

⅓ cup mayonnaise or salad dressing

3 tablespoons Dijon mustard

½ teaspoon pepper

2 cloves garlic, crushed

1 pound new potatoes, each cut into 6 wedges

Chopped fresh chives, if desired

Heat oven to 325°. Line broiler pan with aluminum foil. Spray rack of broiler pan with nonstick cooking spray. Place chicken, skin sides up, on rack in broiler pan. Mix mayonnaise, mustard, pepper and garlic in large bowl; brush about 3 tablespoons mixture on chicken. Cover and refrigerate remaining mayonnaise mixture. Bake uncovered 30 minutes.

Arrange chicken in center of rack in broiler pan. Cover chicken with aluminum foil. Add potatoes to remaining mayonnaise mixture; toss. Arrange potatoes around chicken. (Do not cover potatoes with foil). Bake about 45 minutes, turning potatoes halfway through, until juice of chicken is no longer pink when centers of thickest pieces are cut and potatoes are tender. Sprinkle with chives. *6 servings.*

NUTRITION INFORMATION PER SERVING

1 serving		Percent of U.S. RDA	
Calories	365	Vitamin A	2%
Protein, g	28	Vitamin C	4%
Carbohydrate, g	15	Calcium	4%
Fat, g	22	Iron	10%
Cholesterol, mg	90		
Sodium, mg	240		

How to Poach Chicken

Use poached chicken in salads, casseroles and other recipes. Use this method when you don't need the broth.

2½- to 3-pound cut-up broiler-fryer chicken
¼ cup water
½ teaspoon salt, if desired

Remove any excess fat from chicken and place water in Dutch oven; sprinkle with salt. Heat to boiling; reduce heat. Cover and simmer 45 to 60 minutes until juice of chicken is no longer pink when centers of thickest pieces are cut. Remove chicken from Dutch oven; cool 10 minutes. Remove chicken from bones and skin. Cover and refrigerate up to 2 days. *3 to 4 cups cut-up cooked chicken.*

Chile Chicken with Southwest Relish

Southwest Relish (below)

1 teaspoon chile powder

½ teaspoon paprika

3- to 3½-pound cut-up broiler-fryer chicken

Heat oven to 375°. Prepare Southwest Relish. Mix chile powder and paprika; sprinkle over chicken. Place chicken, skin sides down, in ungreased rectangular pan, 13×9×2 inches. Bake uncovered 30 minutes; turn chicken. Bake about 35 minutes longer or until juice of chicken is no longer pink when centers of thickest pieces are cut. Serve with relish. *6 servings.*

SOUTHWEST RELISH

1 cup whole kernel corn

⅔ cup chopped red onion

¼ cup chopped fresh cilantro

3 tablespoons lime juice

1 tablespoon olive or vegetable oil

1 medium avocado, cut into bite-size pieces

1 clove garlic, finely chopped

1 can (15 ounces) black beans, rinsed and drained

Mix all ingredients. Cover and refrigerate at least 1 hour to blend flavors.

TO GRILL: Mix chile powder and paprika; sprinkle over chicken. Cover and grill chicken, skin sides up, 4 to 6 inches from medium coals 15 minutes; turn chicken. Cover and grill 20 to 40 minutes longer, turning occasionally, until juice of chicken is no longer pink when centers of thickest pieces are cut.

NUTRITION INFORMATION PER SERVING

1 serving		Percent of U.S. RDA	
Calories	390	Vitamin A	8%
Protein, g	34	Vitamin C	10%
Carbohydrate, g	29	Calcium	8%
Fat, g	19	Iron	22%
Cholesterol, mg	85		
Sodium, mg	340		

CHAPTER
3

Breasts

Chicken breasts are the hands down favorites of cooks of all kind. Skinless boneless chicken breasts are easy to buy, and make the perfect starting point for an array of tempting dishes, such as Pear-Potato Chicken Soup, Fresh Berry–Chicken Salad and Cornmeal Chicken with Peach Salsa. There are also wonderful recipes for turkey breast, such as Stuffed Turkey Tenderloins and Grilled Turkey Breast with Plum Sauce. Or, if you'd like to bone your own chicken breasts, you can see page xi for complete instructions.

We've also included an entire section of quick chicken marinades, along with instructions for how to broil, grill or cook your marinated chicken on the stovetop. You'll find enough marinades for an entire work-day week of zesty chicken breasts!

Tequila Chicken with Fettucine (page 87)

Chicken–Black Bean Nachos

1 package (6 ounces) tortilla chips

1 can (15 ounces) black beans, rinsed and drained

½ pound cooked skinless boneless chicken breasts, shredded

1 cup shredded Monterey Jack cheese (4 ounces)

¼ cup pickled jalapeño chiles, drained

½ cup guacamole

½ cup salsa

Heat oven to 350°. Place tortilla chips on ungreased cookie sheet. Top with beans, chicken, cheese and chiles. Bake 3 to 5 minutes or until cheese is melted. Top with guacamole and salsa. *6 servings.*

NUTRITION INFORMATION PER SERVING

1 serving		Percent of U.S. RDA	
Calories	375	Vitamin A	12%
Protein, g	24	Vitamin C	10%
Carbohydrate, g	41	Calcium	20%
Fat, g	16	Iron	20%
Cholesterol, mg	45		
Sodium, mg	910		

Black and White Chili

1 tablespoon vegetable oil

1½ pounds turkey breast tenderloins, cut into ½-inch cubes

1 cup chopped onion (about 1 medium)

½ cup chopped fresh Anaheim or poblano chiles

1 clove garlic, finely chopped

1 cup chopped tomato (about 1 large)

3 cups chicken broth

1 tablespoon chile powder

1 can (15 ounces) black beans, rinsed and drained

1 can (15 to 16 ounces) cannellini beans, rinsed and drained

Heat oil in 3-quart saucepan over medium-high heat until hot. Cook turkey, onion, chiles and garlic in oil, stirring occasionally, until onion is tender and turkey is no longer pink in center. Stir in remaining ingredients. Heat to boiling; reduce heat. Cover and simmer 30 minutes, stirring occasionally. *6 servings.*

NUTRITION INFORMATION PER SERVING

1 serving		Percent of U.S. RDA	
Calories	365	Vitamin A	6%
Protein, g	43	Vitamin C	14%
Carbohydrate, g	42	Calcium	14%
Fat, g	7	Iron	34%
Cholesterol, mg	65		
Sodium, mg	940		

Pear-Potato Chicken Soup

You'll find this a comforting soup for autumn or winter. If you'd like to add color, use red potatoes and red pears with the skins on.

1 tablespoon margarine or butter

1 pound skinless boneless chicken breasts, cubed

½ cup chopped onion (about 1 medium)

2 cups cubed red potatoes (about 2 medium)

2 cups cubed pears (about 2 medium)

½ cup chopped celery (about 1 medium stalk)

1 can (14½ ounces) ready-to-serve chicken broth

2 cups milk

¼ teaspoon salt

½ teaspoon ground nutmeg

Heat margarine in 3-quart saucepan over medium-high heat until melted. Cook chicken and onion in margarine 8 to 10 minutes, stirring occasionally, until chicken is no longer pink in center. Stir in potatoes, pears, celery and broth. Heat to boiling; reduce heat. Cover and simmer about 12 minutes or until potatoes are tender. Stir in remaining ingredients. Cook over low heat about 5 minutes or until hot. Garnish with sliced pear and additional ground nutmeg if desired. *4 servings.*

NUTRITION INFORMATION PER SERVING

1 serving		Percent of U.S. RDA	
Calories	340	Vitamin A	10%
Protein, g	32	Vitamin C	10%
Carbohydrate, g	37	Calcium	18%
Fat, g	9	Iron	10%
Cholesterol, mg	70		
Sodium, mg	630		

Italian Chicken-Lentil Soup

1 tablespoon olive or vegetable oil

*1 pound skinless boneless chicken breasts,
    cut into 1-inch pieces*

½ cup chopped onion (about 1 medium)

*2 cups diced yellow summer squash
    (about 2 medium)*

*2 cups thinly sliced carrots (about 4
    medium)*

1 cup sliced mushrooms

1 cup dried lentils, sorted and rinsed

4½ cups chicken broth

*¼ cup chopped fresh or 1 tablespoon
    dried basil leaves*

½ teaspoon salt

¼ teaspoon pepper

*1 can (28 ounces) Italian pear-shaped
    tomatoes, undrained*

Grated Parmesan cheese

Heat oil in Dutch oven over medium-high heat until hot. Cook chicken and onion in oil 10 to 12 minutes, stirring occasionally, until chicken is no longer pink in center. Stir in remaining ingredients except cheese; break up tomatoes. Heat to boiling, stirring occasionally; reduce heat to medium-low. Cover and cook 20 to 25 minutes or until lentils are tender. Serve with cheese. *6 servings.*

NUTRITION INFORMATION PER SERVING

1 serving		*Percent of U.S. RDA*	
Calories	300	Vitamin A	84%
Protein, g	32	Vitamin C	28%
Carbohydrate, g	34	Calcium	12%
Fat, g	7	Iron	32%
Cholesterol, mg	45		
Sodium, mg	1060		

Turkey-Corn Chowder

1 tablespoon vegetable oil

*1 pound turkey breast tenderloins, cut
    into 1-inch pieces*

1 cup sliced leeks

1 cup julienne strips zucchini

1 clove garlic, finely chopped

*¼ cup chopped fresh or 1 tablespoon
    dried dill weed*

½ teaspoon salt

¼ teaspoon pepper

1 cup clam juice or chicken broth

*¾ pound red new potatoes, cut into 1-inch
    pieces*

2 cups half-and-half

½ cup fresh or frozen whole kernel corn

Heat oil in 3-quart saucepan over medium-high heat until hot. Cook turkey, leeks, zucchini and garlic in oil 10 to 12 minutes, stirring occasionally, until turkey is no longer pink in center. Stir in dill weed, salt, pepper, clam juice and potatoes. Reduce heat. Simmer uncovered over low heat 15 to 20 minutes or until potatoes are tender. Stir in remaining ingredients. Cook uncovered about 5 minutes or until hot. *6 servings.*

NUTRITION INFORMATION PER SERVING

1 serving		*Percent of U.S. RDA*	
Calories	290	Vitamin A	10%
Protein, g	23	Vitamin C	10%
Carbohydrate, g	20	Calcium	12%
Fat, g	14	Iron	12%
Cholesterol, mg	75		
Sodium, mg	390		

Italian Chicken-Lentil Soup

Fresh Berry–Chicken Salad

A lovely summertime recipe to make when fresh berries are at their best. Feel free to experiment and use any combination of berries, such as raspberries, blackberries or blueberries.

4 skinless boneless chicken breast halves (about 1 pound)

2½ cups chicken broth

2 tablespoons raspberry vinegar

6 cups bite-size pieces Boston lettuce

½ pint raspberries

½ pint strawberries, cut in half

Raspberry Vinaigrette (right)

Place chicken breast halves, broth and vinegar in 12-inch skillet. Heat to boiling; reduce heat. Cover and simmer about 20 minutes or until juice of chicken is no longer pink when centers of thickest pieces are cut. Refrigerate chicken in broth until cool.

Remove chicken from broth; discard broth. Cut chicken diagonally into ¼-inch slices. Arrange chicken on lettuce. Top with berries. Drizzle Raspberry Vinaigrette over salad. *4 servings.*

RASPBERRY VINAIGRETTE

⅓ cup vegetable oil

2 tablespoons raspberry vinegar

2 tablespoons raspberry jam

Beat all ingredients, using wire whisk.

NUTRITION INFORMATION PER SERVING

1 serving		Percent of U.S. RDA	
Calories	385	Vitamin A	4%
Protein, g	29	Vitamin C	56%
Carbohydrate, g	16	Calcium	4%
Fat, g	23	Iron	12%
Cholesterol, mg	60		
Sodium, mg	550		

Fresh Berry–Chicken Salad

Chicken, Barley and Corn Salad

½ cup uncooked quick-cooking barley

1 package (10 ounces) frozen baby lima beans, thawed

2 teaspoons vegetable oil

1 pound skinless boneless chicken breasts, cut into 1-inch pieces

1 cup chopped red bell pepper (about 1 medium)

1 tablespoon sugar

1 tablespoon all-purpose flour

¼ teaspoon salt

⅓ cup cider vinegar

1 tablespoon chopped fresh or 1 teaspoon dried thyme leaves

1 tablespoon chopped fresh parsley

1 package (10 ounces) frozen whole kernel corn, thawed

Heat 2 cups water to boiling in 2-quart saucepan. Cook barley and lima beans in boiling water 10 to 12 minutes, stirring occasionally, until barley is tender; drain.

Heat oil in 10-inch skillet over medium-high heat until hot. Cook chicken and bell pepper in oil 10 to 15 minutes, stirring occasionally, until chicken is no longer pink in center. Beat sugar, flour, salt and vinegar, using wire whisk; stir into chicken mixture. Cook and stir about 1 minute or until blended. Stir in barley mixture and remaining ingredients. Serve warm. *4 servings.*

NUTRITION INFORMATION PER SERVING

1 serving		Percent of U.S. RDA	
Calories	375	Vitamin A	18%
Protein, g	34	Vitamin C	100%
Carbohydrate, g	55	Calcium	4%
Fat, g	6	Iron	20%
Cholesterol, mg	60		
Sodium, mg	240		

Sesame Chicken Salad

2 teaspoons vegetable oil

4 skinless boneless chicken breast halves (about 1 pound)

4 cups bite-size pieces romaine

1 cup thinly sliced cucumber

1 cup shredded carrots (about 1½ medium)

1 jar (7 ounces) baby corn, drained

Sesame Dressing (below)

Heat oil in 10-inch skillet over medium-high heat until hot. Cook chicken breast halves in oil 15 to 20 minutes, turning once, until juice of chicken is no longer pink when centers of thickest pieces are cut. Prepare Sesame Dressing. Cut chicken diagonally into ½-inch slices. Toss remaining ingredients; place on 6 serving plates. Top with chicken. Serve warm. *6 servings.*

SESAME DRESSING

⅓ cup vegetable oil

¼ cup white vinegar

1 tablespoon sesame seed, toasted

1 teaspoon sesame oil

½ teaspoon sugar

Beat all ingredients, using wire whisk.

TO GRILL: Brush chicken breast halves with oil. Cover and grill 4 to 6 inches from medium coals 15 to 20 minutes, turning once, until juice of chicken is no longer pink when centers of thickest pieces are cut.

NUTRITION INFORMATION PER SERVING

1 serving		Percent of U.S. RDA	
Calories	270	Vitamin A	34%
Protein, g	19	Vitamin C	8%
Carbohydrate, g	10	Calcium	2%
Fat, g	18	Iron	8%
Cholesterol, mg	45		
Sodium, mg	160		

Smoked Turkey with Artichokes

If green peppercorns are not available, you can use capers in the dressing instead. Peppercorns—or capers—give the dressing a lovely flavor that goes nicely with the smoked turkey.

1½ pounds smoked turkey breast, cut into ¾ × ¼-inch pieces

½ cup chopped celery (about 1 medium stalk)

½ cup cubed Jarlsberg or Swiss cheese

¼ cup sliced green onions (2 to 3 medium)

2 cans (14 ounces each) artichoke hearts, drained and cut into fourths

1 package (10 ounces) chopped mixed salad greens (3 cups)

Green Peppercorn Dressing (right)

Mix all ingredients except Green Peppercorn Dressing in large bowl. Prepare dressing, pour over salad; toss. *6 servings.*

GREEN PEPPERCORN DRESSING

½ cup mayonnaise or salad dressing

1 tablespoon chopped fresh or 1 teaspoon dried tarragon leaves

1 tablespoon pickled green peppercorns or capers, if desired, drained

1 tablespoon lemon juice

Mix all ingredients.

NUTRITION INFORMATION PER SERVING

1 serving		*Percent of U.S. RDA*	
Calories	390	Vitamin A	16%
Protein, g	40	Vitamin C	12%
Carbohydrate, g	11	Calcium	14%
Fat, g	22	Iron	16%
Cholesterol, mg	105		
Sodium, mg	410		

Chicken Salad Florentine

If you don't have fresh basil, increase the amount of spinach by about ½ cup and use 1 teaspoon dried basil leaves in the Pine Nut Dressing.

Pine Nut Dressing (right)

6 skinless boneless chicken breast halves (about 1½ pounds)

1 tablespoon vegetable oil

6 cups bite-size pieces spinach (about 4 ounces)

½ cup fresh basil leaves, cut into strips

¼ cup sliced ripe olives

¼ cup pine nuts, toasted

Prepare Pine Nut Dressing. Flatten chicken breast halves to ¼-inch thickness between plastic wrap or waxed paper. Heat oil in 10-inch skillet over medium-high heat until hot. Cook chicken in oil 10 to 12 minutes, turning once, until juice of chicken is no longer pink when centers of thickest pieces are cut. Mix remaining ingredients; place on 6 serving plates. Top each serving with a chicken breast half. Drizzle with dressing. *6 servings.*

PINE NUT DRESSING

3 tablespoons pine nuts

1 clove garlic

1 tablespoon red wine vinegar

¼ cup olive or vegetable oil

½ teaspoon salt

Place pine nuts and garlic in blender or food processor. Cover and blend, or process, until finely ground. Add vinegar, oil and salt. Cover and blend, or process, until well blended.

TO GRILL: Flatten chicken breast halves as directed; brush with oil. Cover and grill 4 to 6 inches from medium coals 10 to 15 minutes, turning once, until juice of chicken is no longer pink when centers of thickest pieces are cut.

NUTRITION INFORMATION PER SERVING

1 serving		Percent of U.S. RDA	
Calories	315	Vitamin A	50%
Protein, g	29	Vitamin C	14%
Carbohydrate, g	6	Calcium	12%
Fat, g	21	Iron	22%
Cholesterol, mg	65		
Sodium, mg	340		

Chicken Tabbouleh Salad

Traditional tabbouleh salad is made with cracked wheat or bulgur as a base. Our salad uses couscous to create a lighter texture.

1 cup chicken broth

1 pound skinless boneless chicken breasts, cut into ½-inch pieces

½ cup uncooked couscous

1 cup chopped cucumber (about 1 small)

½ cup finely chopped onion (about 1 medium)

½ cup chopped tomato (about 1 small)

½ cup chopped fresh parsley

¼ cup lime juice

2 tablespoons chopped fresh mint leaves

2 tablespoons vegetable oil

½ teaspoon salt

Heat broth to boiling in 2-quart saucepan. Stir in chicken. Cook over medium heat 10 to 15 minutes or until chicken is no longer pink in center. Stir in couscous; remove from heat. Cover and let stand 5 to 10 minutes or until liquid is absorbed. Mix chicken mixture and remaining ingredients in large glass or plastic bowl. Cover and refrigerate 1 hour to blend flavors. *4 servings.*

NUTRITION INFORMATION PER SERVING

1 serving		Percent of U.S. RDA	
Calories	300	Vitamin A	6%
Protein, g	29	Vitamin C	16%
Carbohydrate, g	23	Calcium	4%
Fat, g	11	Iron	10%
Cholesterol, mg	60		
Sodium, mg	530		

Hot Chicken Salad with Plum Sauce

2 teaspoons olive or vegetable oil

4 skinless boneless chicken breast halves (about 1 pound)

1 can (16 ounces) purple plums in juice, rinsed, drained and pitted

1 tablespoon lemon juice

2 teaspoons packed brown sugar

¼ teaspoon ground ginger

⅛ teaspoon crushed red pepper

1 clove garlic

4 cups shredded Napa (Chinese) cabbage

1 cup bean sprouts (about 2 ounces)

1 tablespoon thinly sliced green onion

Heat oil in 10-inch nonstick skillet over medium-high heat. Cook chicken breast halves in oil 15 to 20 minutes, turning once, until juice is no longer pink when centers of thickest pieces are cut.

Place remaining ingredients except cabbage, bean sprouts and onion in blender or food processor. Cover and blend on high speed or process about 30 seconds until smooth. Heat sauce if desired.

Arrange cabbage, bean sprouts and onion on 4 serving plates. Top with chicken. Spoon plum sauce over chicken. *4 servings.*

NUTRITION INFORMATION PER SERVING

1 serving		Percent of U.S. RDA	
Calories	245	Vitamin A	24%
Protein, g	28	Vitamin C	30%
Carbohydrate, g	17	Calcium	10%
Fat, g	7	Iron	12%
Cholesterol, mg	60		
Sodium, mg	110		

Chicken BLT Sandwiches

2 teaspoons vegetable oil

4 skinless boneless chicken breast halves (about 1 pound)

¼ cup bacon-and-tomato or Thousand Island dressing

4 whole wheat sandwich buns, split

8 slices tomato

4 slices bacon, cooked

4 lettuce leaves

Heat oil in 10-inch skillet over medium-high heat until hot. Cook chicken breast halves in oil 15 to 20 minutes, turning once, until juice of chicken is no longer pink when centers of thickest pieces are cut. Spread dressing on cut sides of buns. Layer chicken, tomato, bacon and lettuce on bottoms of buns. Top with tops of buns. *4 sandwiches.*

TO GRILL: Brush chicken breast halves with oil. Cover and grill 4 to 6 inches from medium coals 15 to 20 minutes, turning once, until juice of chicken is no longer pink when centers of thickest pieces are cut.

NUTRITION INFORMATION PER SERVING

1 sandwich		Percent of U.S. RDA	
Calories	353	Vitamin A	6%
Protein, g	32	Vitamin C	10%
Carbohydrate, g	20	Calcium	6%
Fat, g	17	Iron	14%
Cholesterol, mg	75		
Sodium, mg	470		

Cajun Chicken Sandwiches

Cajun food hails from Louisiana but has French roots. It is simple hearty country French food that was adapted by the Acadians of Louisiana, using hot peppers, garlic and other native ingredients.

1 teaspoon fennel seed, crushed

½ teaspoon garlic salt

¼ teaspoon white pepper

¼ teaspoon ground red pepper (cayenne)

4 skinless boneless chicken breast halves (about 1 pound)

2 teaspoons vegetable oil

4 kaiser rolls, split

4 slices (1 ounce each) Monterey Jack cheese with jalapeño peppers

Mix fennel seed, garlic salt, white pepper and red pepper. Rub chicken breast halves with fennel seed mixture. Heat oil in 10-inch skillet over medium-high heat. Cook chicken in oil 15 to 20 minutes, turning once, until juice of chicken is no longer pink when centers of thickest pieces are cut. Place one chicken breast half on bottom of each roll. Top each with 1 slice cheese and top of roll. *4 sandwiches.*

NUTRITION INFORMATION PER SERVING

1 sandwich		Percent of U.S. RDA	
Calories	405	Vitamin A	8%
Protein, g	37	Vitamin C	*
Carbohydrate, g	30	Calcium	24%
Fat, g	16	Iron	14%
Cholesterol, mg	95		
Sodium, mg	670		

Chicken-Pesto Sandwiches

Foccacia bread is an Italian flat bread available in many varieties. You'll find it topped with fresh herbs or onions or tomatoes and brushed with olive oil. Pick the variety you like best for this Italian-inspired sandwich.

6 skinless boneless chicken breast halves (about 1½ pounds)

½ teaspoon salt

2 tablespoons chopped fresh or 2 teaspoons dried oregano leaves

1 loaf Italian focaccia bread (about 10 inches in diameter)

1½ cups shredded spinach (about ¾ ounce)

1 container (7 ounces) refrigerated pesto sauce

6 slices tomato

Flatten chicken breast halves to ¼-inch thickness between plastic wrap or waxed paper. Sprinkle with salt and oregano. Set oven control to broil.

Place chicken on rack in broiler pan. Broil with tops 4 to 6 inches from heat 15 to 20 minutes, turning once, until juice of chicken is no longer pink when centers of thickest pieces are cut. Cut bread horizontally in half. Cut up into 6 wedges. Spread bread bottom with pesto. Layer chicken, spinach, and tomato on bottom wedges. Top with top wedges. *6 sandwiches.*

TO GRILL: Flatten chicken breast halves as directed; sprinkle with salt and oregano. Cover and grill 4 to 6 inches from medium coals 10 to 15 minutes, turning once, until juice of chicken is no longer pink when centers of thickest pieces are cut.

NUTRITION INFORMATION PER SERVING

1 sandwich		*Percent of U.S. RDA*	
Calories	575	Vitamin A	16%
Protein, g	35	Vitamin C	6%
Carbohydrate, g	37	Calcium	18%
Fat, g	33	Iron	26%
Cholesterol, mg	70		
Sodium, mg	1190		

Chicken-Pesto Sandwiches

Chicken–Cream Cheese Bagels

2 teaspoons vegetable oil

1 pound skinless boneless chicken breasts, cut into ½-inch pieces

¼ cup chopped green onions (2 to 3 medium)

1 tablespoon chopped ripe olives

1 container (8 ounces) soft cream cheese

6 bagels, split

Heat oil in 10-inch skillet over medium-high heat until hot. Cook chicken in oil 10 to 15 minutes, stirring occasionally, until chicken is no longer pink in center. Remove from skillet. Mix chicken, green onions, olives and cream cheese. Set oven control to broil. Spread about 2 tablespoons chicken mixture on each bagel half. Place on rack in broiler pan. Broil with tops 6 inches from heat 3 to 5 minutes or until hot. *12 sandwiches.*

NUTRITION INFORMATION PER SERVING

2 sandwiches		Percent of U.S. RDA	
Calories	360	Vitamin A	10%
Protein, g	24	Vitamin C	*
Carbohydrate, g	31	Calcium	6%
Fat, g	16	Iron	18%
Cholesterol, mg	75		
Sodium, mg	360		

Chicken-Apple Sandwiches

2 teaspoons vegetable oil

1 pound skinless boneless chicken breasts, cut into ½-inch strips

1 cup chopped all-purpose apple (about 1 medium)

½ cup finely chopped celery (about 1 medium stalk)

¼ cup chopped pecans

¼ cup shredded Cheddar cheese (1 ounce)

¼ cup mayonnaise or salad dressing

4 sourdough rolls, split

Heat oil in 10-inch skillet over medium-high heat until hot. Cook chicken in oil 10 to 12 minutes, stirring occasionally, until chicken is no longer pink in center. Stir in remaining ingredients except rolls. Cook about 5 minutes, stirring occasionally, until hot. Fill rolls with chicken mixture. *4 sandwiches.*

NUTRITION INFORMATION PER SERVING

1 sandwich		Percent of U.S. RDA	
Calories	460	Vitamin A	2%
Protein, g	31	Vitamin C	2%
Carbohydrate, g	32	Calcium	10%
Fat, g	24	Iron	14%
Cholesterol, mg	80		
Sodium, mg	460		

Grilled Chicken on Black Bread

Russian rye bread is typically very dark and sometimes even includes cocoa or coffee in the ingredients. If it's unavailable, you can substitute light rye or whole wheat.

4 skinless boneless chicken breast halves (about 1 pound)

2 teaspoons vegetable oil

½ cup Russian dressing

8 slices Russian rye bread

¼ cup chopped walnuts

1 small bunch watercress

Flatten chicken breast halves to ¼-inch thickness between plastic wrap or waxed paper. Brush with oil. Cover and grill 4 to 6 inches from medium coals 10 to 15 minutes, turning once, until juice of chicken is no longer pink when centers of thickest pieces are cut. Spread 1 tablespoon dressing over each slice bread. Place 1 chicken breast half on each of 4 slices bread. Top with walnuts, watercress and remaining bread. *4 sandwiches.*

TO SAUTÉ: Flatten chicken breast halves as directed; do not brush with oil. Heat oil in 10-inch skillet over medium-high heat until hot. Cook chicken in oil 10 to 12 minutes, turning once, until juice of chicken is no longer pink when centers of thickest pieces are cut.

NUTRITION INFORMATION PER SERVING

1 sandwich		*Percent of U.S. RDA*	
Calories	485	Vitamin A	6%
Protein, g	32	Vitamin C	4%
Carbohydrate, g	30	Calcium	8%
Fat, g	28	Iron	16%
Cholesterol, mg	70		
Sodium, mg	690		

Broiled Chicken-Cheese Sandwiches

2 teaspoons vegetable oil

1 pound skinless boneless chicken breasts

1 cup shredded Cheddar cheese (4 ounces)

¼ cup mayonnaise or salad dressing

¼ cup chopped green onions (2 to 3 medium)

4 slices bacon, crisply cooked and crumbled

1 baguette (14 to 16 inches), cut horizontally in half

Heat oil in 10-inch skillet over medium-high heat until hot. Cook chicken breasts in oil 15 to 20 minutes, turning once, until juice of chicken is no longer pink when centers of thickest pieces are cut. Shred chicken into small pieces. Mix chicken and remaining ingredients except baguette. Spread chicken mixture over each baguette half. Set oven control to broil. Place baguette halves on rack in broiler pan. Broil with tops about 6 inches from heat 3 to 5 minutes or until cheese is melted and chicken mixture is hot. Cut each baguette half into 2 pieces. *4 open-face sandwiches.*

NUTRITION INFORMATION PER SERVING

1 sandwich		*Percent of U.S. RDA*	
Calories	595	Vitamin A	6%
Protein, g	42	Vitamin C	2%
Carbohydrate, g	41	Calcium	22%
Fat, g	30	Iron	20%
Cholesterol, mg	110		
Sodium, mg	830		

Chicken Quesadilla Sandwiches

2 teaspoons vegetable oil

1 pound skinless boneless chicken breasts

¼ cup chopped fresh cilantro

¼ teaspoon ground cumin

8 flour tortillas (8 inches in diameter)

2 tablespoons vegetable oil

1 cup shredded Monterey Jack cheese (4 ounces)

1 can (4 ounces) chopped green chiles, drained

Heat 2 teaspoons oil in 10-inch skillet over medium-high heat until hot. Cook chicken breasts, cilantro and cumin in oil 15 to 20 minutes, turning chicken once and stirring cilantro mixture occasionally, until juice of chicken is no longer pink when centers of thickest pieces are cut. Shred chicken into small pieces; mix chicken and cilantro mixture.

Brush 1 side of 1 tortilla with some of the 2 tablespoons oil; place oil side down in same skillet. Layer with one-fourth of the chicken mixture, ¼ cup of the cheese and one-fourth of the chiles to within ½ inch of edge of tortilla. Top with another tortilla; brush top of tortilla with oil. Cook over medium-high heat 4 to 6 minutes, turning after 2 minutes, until light golden brown. Repeat with remaining tortillas, chicken mixture, cheese and chiles. Cut quesadillas into wedges. Serve with salsa if desired. *4 servings.*

TO GRILL: Assemble quesadillas on platter, brushing outer sides of tortillas generously with oil. Carefully slide onto grill. Grill uncovered 4 to 6 inches from medium coals 4 to 6 minutes, turning after 2 minutes, until light golden brown.

NUTRITION INFORMATION PER SERVING

1 serving		*Percent of U.S. RDA*	
Calories	575	Vitamin A	12%
Protein, g	37	Vitamin C	20%
Carbohydrate, g	48	Calcium	28%
Fat, g	27	Iron	26%
Cholesterol, mg	95		
Sodium, mg	890		

Chicken Quesadilla Sandwiches

Chicken Piccata

6 skinless boneless chicken breast halves (about 1½ pounds)

1 egg, slightly beaten

1 tablespoon water

½ cup dry bread crumbs

½ teaspoon salt

¼ teaspoon pepper

⅛ teaspoon garlic powder

¼ cup all-purpose flour

2 tablespoons margarine or butter

2 tablespoons vegetable oil

2 tablespoons lemon juice

2 tablespoons dry white wine or chicken broth

Flatten chicken breast halves to ¼-inch thickness between plastic wrap or waxed paper. Mix egg and water. Mix bread crumbs, salt, pepper and garlic powder. Coat chicken with flour. Dip into egg mixture; coat with bread crumb mixture.

Heat margarine and oil in 12-inch skillet over medium heat until hot. Cook chicken in margarine mixture 8 to 10 minutes, turning once, until juice of chicken is no longer pink when centers of thickest pieces are cut. Remove chicken from skillet using tongs; keep warm. Stir lemon juice and wine into drippings in skillet. Heat to boiling; pour over chicken. Sprinkle with chopped fresh parsley and serve with lemon wedges if desired. *6 servings.*

NUTRITION INFORMATION PER SERVING

1 serving		*Percent of U.S. RDA*	
Calories	275	Vitamin A	6%
Protein, g	29	Vitamin C	*
Carbohydrate, g	11	Calcium	2%
Fat, g	13	Iron	10%
Cholesterol, mg	100		
Sodium, mg	360		

Tequila Chicken with Fettuccine

Toss fettuccine with 1 teaspoon of the grated lime peel to add vibrant color.

¼ cup tequila or chicken broth

¼ cup frozen (thawed) limeade

1 tablespoon grated lime peel

1½ pounds skinless boneless chicken breasts, cut into 1½×½-inch strips

1 small orange or yellow bell pepper, cut into ¼-inch strips

1½ cups sliced mushrooms

1 clove garlic, finely chopped

1 package (16 ounces) spinach fettuccine

½ cup grated Parmesan cheese

Mix tequila, limeade and lime peel in medium glass or plastic bowl. Stir in chicken. Cover and refrigerate 30 minutes.

Place chicken and marinade in 12-inch skillet. Stir in bell pepper, mushrooms and garlic. Cook over medium-high heat 10 to 12 minutes, stirring occasionally, until chicken is no longer pink in center. Cook fettuccine as directed on package; drain. Place fettuccine on 6 serving plates. Spoon chicken mixture over fettuccine. Sprinkle with cheese. Garnish with grated lime peel if desired. *6 servings.*

NUTRITION INFORMATION PER SERVING

1 serving		Percent of U.S. RDA	
Calories	440	Vitamin A	6%
Protein, g	37	Vitamin C	14%
Carbohydrate, g	55	Calcium	12%
Fat, g	8	Iron	24%
Cholesterol, mg	130		
Sodium, mg	510		

Poultry Yields

CUBED, CHOPPED OR SHREDDED CHICKEN OR TURKEY

Use the following guidelines to determine how much uncooked chicken or turkey is needed when a recipe calls for cubed, chopped or shredded cooked chicken:

- One 3- to 3½-pound broiler-fryer chicken yields about 2½ to 3 cups.

- 1½ pounds of whole bone-in chicken breast yield about 2 cups.

- 1½ pounds of skinless boneless chicken breast or turkey tenderloins yield about 3 cups.

- 1½ pounds of chicken hindquarters (thigh and drumstick) yield about 1¾ cups.

- 1½ pounds of whole turkey breast yield about 2½ cups.

- One 6- to 8-pound turkey yields about 7 to 10 cups.

WHOLE CHICKEN OR TURKEY, OR CUT-UP PARTS

As a general rule, when purchasing whole chicken or turkey, or parts, plan for about ¾ pound per person; this includes the weight of the bone.

Quick Chicken Marinades

How do you get a delicious dinner on the table in a hurry? Try combining chicken and a flavorful marinade and freezing in portions suited to your family. Not only do you achieve great flavor and variety but the short preparation and cooking times come in handy on busy days when time is precious.

Prepare Marinade and Chicken:

- Prepare the marinade of your choice from the chart below. Flatten four skinless boneless chicken breast halves or thighs to ¼-inch thickness between plastic wrap or waxed paper.

- Combine chicken and marinade in a sealable, heavy-duty plastic freezer bag. Carefully press air out of bag to reduce freezer burn; seal and label. Refrigerate eight to twenty-four hours or freeze up to two months.

- To prepare, thaw chicken in refrigerator overnight and cook according to one of the methods at right.

Cooking Directions:

Stovetop: Heat 1 teaspoon oil in 10-inch nonstick skillet over medium heat. Add chicken. Cook 8 to 10 minutes, turning once, or until golden brown and juice of chicken is no longer pink when centers of thickest pieces are cut.

Broil: Place chicken on rack in broiler pan. Broil 4 to 6 inches from heat 8 to 10 minutes, turning once, until juice of chicken is no longer pink when centers of thickest pieces are cut.

Grill: Grill 4 to 6 inches from medium coals 10 to 15 minutes, turning once, until juice of chicken is no longer pink when centers of thickest pieces are cut.

Garlic Marinade

3 tablespoons vegetable oil

4 cloves garlic, finely chopped

1 tablespoon chopped fresh or 1 teaspoon dried rosemary leaves, crushed

½ teaspoon ground mustard

2 teaspoons soy sauce

3 tablespoons red or white wine vinegar, dry sherry or apple juice

Heat oil in 10-inch skillet over medium-high heat. Sauté garlic in oil until golden. Stir in rosemary, mustard and soy sauce; remove from heat. Stir in vinegar or sherry; cool. About ½ cup marinade.

Proceed as directed above.

Fajita Marinade

¼ *cup vegetable oil*

¼ *cup red wine vinegar*

1 *tablespoon chopped fresh or 1 teaspoon dried oregano leaves*

1 *teaspoon sugar*

1 *teaspoon chile powder*

½ *teaspoon garlic powder*

½ *teaspoon salt*

¼ *teaspoon pepper*

Mix all ingredients. About ½ cup marinade.

Proceed as directed on opposite page.

Lemon-Herb Marinade

¼ *cup vegetable oil*

3 *tablespoons lemon juice*

1 *tablespoon chopped fresh or 1 teaspoon dried basil leaves*

2 *teaspoons chopped fresh or ½ teaspoon dried thyme leaves*

½ *teaspoon salt*

¼ *teaspoon pepper*

2 *cloves garlic, finely chopped*

Mix all ingredients. About ½ cup marinade.

Proceed as directed on opposite page.

Teriyaki Marinade

¼ *cup water*

1 *tablespoon packed brown sugar*

3 *tablespoons soy sauce*

1 *tablespoon lemon juice*

1 *tablespoon vegetable oil*

⅛ *teaspoon coarsely ground pepper*

1 *clove garlic, finely chopped*

Mix all ingredients. About ½ cup marinade.

Proceed as directed on opposite page.

Super-Easy Marinade

½ *cup bottled marinade or salad dressing*

Proceed as directed on opposite page.

Grilled Chicken Kabobs with Dipping Sauce

¼ cup vegetable oil

2 tablespoons white vinegar

1 tablespoon soy sauce

1 pound skinless boneless chicken breasts, cut into 1-inch cubes

1 small red or yellow bell pepper, cut into 1-inch squares

2 plums, nectarines or peaches, pitted and cut into 1-inch pieces

Dipping Sauce (right)

Mix oil, vinegar and soy sauce in small glass or plastic bowl. Stir in chicken until coated with marinade. Cover and refrigerate 1 hour.

Remove chicken from marinade; reserve marinade. Thread chicken, bell pepper and plum pieces alternately on each of six 12-inch metal skewers, leaving space between each piece. Cover and grill kabobs 4 to 6 inches from medium coals 10 to 15 minutes, turning and brushing 2 or 3 times with marinade, until chicken is no longer pink in center. Discard any remaining marinade. Serve kabobs with Dipping Sauce. *6 servings.*

Dɪᴘᴘɪɴɢ Sᴀᴜᴄᴇ

¼ cup plum jam

1 tablespoon white vinegar

½ teaspoon ground ginger

Mix all ingredients.

Tᴏ ʙʀᴏɪʟ: Set oven control to broil. Place kabobs on rack in broiler pan. Broil with tops 4 to 6 inches from heat 10 to 15 minutes, turning and brushing twice with marinade, until chicken is no longer pink in center. Discard any remaining marinade.

Nᴜᴛʀɪᴛɪᴏɴ Iɴꜰᴏʀᴍᴀᴛɪᴏɴ Pᴇʀ Sᴇʀᴠɪɴɢ

1 serving		*Percent of U.S. RDA*	
Calories	220	Vitamin A	4%
Protein, g	17	Vitamin C	14%
Carbohydrate, g	13	Calcium	*
Fat, g	11	Iron	4%
Cholesterol, mg	40		
Sodium, mg	210		

Jamaican Jerk Chicken

The tradition of "jerking" meat is unique to Jamaica. Originally, the hot spicy seasonings were applied to wild boar to make it more edible. The tradition was then extended to meat and chicken. This recipe is spicy, hot and very colorful with its papaya, mango, red onion and yellow pepper.

2 tablespoons chopped fresh or 2 teaspoons dried thyme leaves

½ teaspoon crushed red pepper

½ teaspoon salt

¼ teaspoon ground allspice

4 skinless boneless chicken breast halves (about 1 pound)

1 cup sliced papaya

1 cup sliced mango

1 medium red onion, sliced

1 medium yellow bell pepper, cut into ¼-inch strips

Heat oven to 375°. Mix thyme, red pepper, salt and allspice. Rub chicken breast halves with thyme mixture. Place chicken in greased rectangular pan, 13×9×2 inches. Cover and bake 30 minutes. Turn chicken; arrange remaining ingredients around chicken in pan. Bake uncovered 20 to 30 minutes longer or until juice of chicken is no longer pink when centers of thickest pieces are cut. *4 servings.*

NUTRITION INFORMATION PER SERVING

1 serving		*Percent of U.S. RDA*	
Calories	190	Vitamin A	28%
Protein, g	27	Vitamin C	58%
Carbohydrate, g	15	Calcium	4%
Fat, g	4	Iron	12%
Cholesterol, mg	65		
Sodium, mg	330		

Fiesta Chicken Breasts

Fresh Tomato Salsa (right)*

4 chicken breast halves

¼ cup lime juice

¼ cup vegetable oil

½ teaspoon ground cumin

½ teaspoon salt

2 tablespoons vegetable oil

4 flour tortillas (8 inches in diameter),
halved and cut into ½-inch strips

Mix all Salsa ingredients in glass or plastic bowl. Refrigerate until ready to serve.

Place chicken breast halves in shallow glass or plastic dish. Mix lime juice, ¼ cup oil, the cumin and salt; pour over chicken. Cover and refrigerate 1 hour.

Heat oven to 375°. Place chicken, skin sides up, in greased square pan, 9×9×2 inches. Pour marinade over chicken. Cover and bake 30 minutes. Uncover and bake 20 to 30 minutes longer, turning chicken after 10 minutes, until juice of chicken is no longer pink when centers of thickest pieces are cut.

Heat 2 tablespoons oil in 10-inch skillet over medium-high heat until hot. Cook tortilla strips in oil 3 to 5 minutes, stirring occasionally, until crisp and golden brown. Mix avocado and salsa. Serve chicken topped with salsa mixture and tortilla strips. *4 servings.*

FRESH TOMATO SALSA

2 medium tomatoes, seeded and chopped
(about 1½ cups)

½ cup chopped avocado

¼ cup sliced green onion (with tops)

1 to 2 tablespoons lime juice

1½ teaspoons finely chopped jalapeño

1 clove garlic, finely chopped

¼ teaspoon salt

TO GRILL: Marinate chicken as directed; drain chicken, reserving marinade. Cover and grill chicken, skin sides up, 4 to 6 inches from medium coals 20 to 25 minutes, turning once and brushing frequently with marinade, until juice of chicken is no longer pink when centers of thickest pieces are cut. Discard any remaining marinade. Place tortilla strips on aluminum foil; brush with oil. Grill tortilla strips 5 to 8 minutes or until crisp.

* 1 cup purchased thick and chunky salsa can be substituted for the Fresh Tomato Salsa. Stir ½ cup chopped avocado into purchased salsa.

NUTRITION INFORMATION PER SERVING

1 serving		Percent of U.S. RDA	
Calories	570	Vitamin A	8%
Protein, g	32	Vitamin C	20%
Carbohydrate, g	30	Calcium	6%
Fat, g	36	Iron	20%
Cholesterol, mg	80		
Sodium, mg	640		

Fiesta Chicken Breasts

Barbecued Chicken with Corn Muffins

Barbecue Sauce (below)

2 teaspoons vegetable oil

1½ pounds skinless boneless chicken breasts, cut into ½-inch strips

4 corn muffins, split

Prepare Barbecue Sauce. Heat oil in 10-inch skillet over medium-high heat until hot. Cook chicken in oil 10 to 15 minutes, stirring occasionally, until chicken is no longer pink in center. Stir in sauce. Spoon chicken mixture over muffins. *4 servings.*

BARBECUE SAUCE

1 cup chopped red onion (about 1 medium)

1 cup ketchup

¾ cup water

¼ cup cider vinegar

1 tablespoon packed brown sugar

1 tablespoon Worcestershire sauce

Mix all ingredients in 1-quart saucepan. Cook over medium heat about 10 minutes, stirring occasionally, until onion is tender.

TO GRILL: Prepare Barbecue Sauce. Place chicken strips on aluminum foil or in hinged wire grill basket. Cover and grill 4 to 6 inches from medium coals 5 to 6 minutes, turning and brushing frequently with sauce, until chicken is no longer pink in center.

Heat remaining sauce to boiling; boil 1 minute, stirring frequently. Mix chicken and sauce. Spoon chicken mixture over muffins.

NUTRITION INFORMATION PER SERVING

1 serving		*Percent of U.S. RDA*	
Calories	415	Vitamin A	8%
Protein, g	40	Vitamin C	10%
Carbohydrate, g	41	Calcium	10%
Fat, g	11	Iron	18%
Cholesterol, mg	110		
Sodium, mg	1020		

Cornmeal Chicken with Peach Salsa

Chicken breasts coated with cornmeal and served with Peach Salsa brings to mind Southern flavors. Try rounding out the meal with flaky southern biscuits.

½ cup yellow cornmeal

½ teaspoon salt

¼ teaspoon pepper

4 skinless boneless chicken breast halves (about 1 pound)

2 tablespoons vegetable oil

Peach Salsa (right)

Mix cornmeal, salt and pepper. Coat chicken breast halves with cornmeal mixture. Heat oil in 10-inch skillet over medium-high heat until hot. Cook chicken in oil 15 to 20 minutes, turning once, until juice of chicken is no longer pink when centers of thickest pieces are cut. Serve with Peach Salsa. *4 servings.*

PEACH SALSA

3 cups chopped peeled fresh peaches*

1 cup chopped tomato (about 1 large)

¼ cup chopped fresh cilantro

3 tablespoons vegetable oil

2 tablespoons white vinegar

¼ teaspoon salt

Mix all ingredients.

* 3 cups chopped frozen (thawed) sliced peaches can be substituted for the fresh peaches.

NUTRITION INFORMATION PER SERVING

1 serving		Percent of U.S. RDA	
Calories	415	Vitamin A	12%
Protein, g	29	Vitamin C	18%
Carbohydrate, g	30	Calcium	2%
Fat, g	21	Iron	12%
Cholesterol, mg	65		
Sodium, mg	470		

Spicy Chicken and Shrimp

1 pound skinless boneless chicken breasts, cut into ¾-inch pieces

1 pound raw medium shrimp, peeled and deveined

1 cup chopped yellow bell pepper (about 1 medium)

1 tablespoon olive or vegetable oil

½ teaspoon salt

¼ teaspoon pepper

¼ teaspoon crushed red pepper

2 jalapeño chiles, seeded and chopped

2 cups chopped tomatoes (about 2 large)

2 cups hot cooked rice

Cook all ingredients except tomatoes and rice in 12-inch skillet over medium-high heat 10 to 15 minutes, stirring occasionally, until chicken is no longer pink in center. Stir in tomatoes. Cook about 1 minute, stirring occasionally, until hot. Serve over rice. *4 servings.*

NUTRITION INFORMATION PER SERVING

1 serving		Percent of U.S. RDA	
Calories	395	Vitamin A	46%
Protein, g	46	Vitamin C	92%
Carbohydrate, g	37	Calcium	6%
Fat, g	8	Iron	30%
Cholesterol, mg	220		
Sodium, mg	910		

Lemon-Pistachio Chicken

4 skinless boneless chicken breast halves (about 1 pound)

1 teaspoon lemon pepper

1 tablespoon vegetable oil

3 tablespoons lemon juice

1 teaspoon grated lemon peel

¼ cup chopped pistachio nuts, toasted

Lemon slices

Flatten chicken breast halves to ¼-inch thickness between plastic wrap or waxed paper. Sprinkle both sides of chicken with lemon pepper. Heat oil in 10-inch skillet over medium-high heat until hot. Cook chicken, lemon juice and lemon peel in oil 15 to 20 minutes, turning chicken once and stirring juice mixture occasionally, until juice of chicken is no longer pink when centers of thickest pieces are cut. Serve chicken topped with juice mixture, nuts and lemon slices. *4 servings.*

NUTRITION INFORMATION PER SERVING

1 serving		Percent of U.S. RDA	
Calories	215	Vitamin A	*
Protein, g	27	Vitamin C	2%
Carbohydrate, g	3	Calcium	2%
Fat, g	11	Iron	8%
Cholesterol, mg	65		
Sodium, mg	130		

Curried Chicken Kabobs

*1 pound skinless boneless chicken breasts,
   cut into 1-inch cubes*

Curry Marinade (below)

2 cups cubed pineapple

2 cups cubed papaya

2 cups 1-inch pieces green bell pepper

Place chicken in shallow glass or plastic dish.
Prepare Curry Marinade; pour over chicken.
Cover and refrigerate 30 minutes.

Set oven control to broil. Remove chicken from
marinade; reserve marinade. Thread chicken,
pineapple, papaya and bell pepper pieces alternately on each of four 15-inch metal skewers,
leaving space between each piece. Place on rack
in broiler pan. Broil with tops 4 to 6 inches from
heat 10 to 15 minutes, turning and brushing frequently with marinade, until chicken is no longer
pink in center. Discard any remaining marinade.
4 servings.

CURRY MARINADE

3 tablespoons lime juice

2 tablespoons honey

1 tablespoon vegetable oil

2 teaspoons curry powder

Beat all ingredients, using wire whisk.

TO GRILL: Cover and grill kabobs 4 to 6 inches
from medium coals 10 to 15 minutes, turning and
brushing frequently with marinade, until chicken
is no longer pink in center. Discard any remaining
marinade.

NUTRITION INFORMATION PER SERVING

1 serving		Percent of U.S. RDA	
Calories	270	Vitamin A	6%
Protein, g	26	Vitamin C	84%
Carbohydrate, g	30	Calcium	4%
Fat, g	7	Iron	10%
Cholesterol, mg	65		
Sodium, mg	65		

Chicken with Glazed Apples

Sliced apples and white wine flavor this dish, based on German cuisine. It's nice served with spaetzel and red cabbage.

4 skinless boneless chicken breast halves (about 1 pound)

½ teaspoon ground nutmeg

¼ teaspoon salt

1 tablespoon vegetable oil

2 cups sliced all-purpose apples (about 2 medium)

¼ cup dry white wine or apple juice

½ cup apple jelly

Sprinkle chicken breast halves with nutmeg and salt. Heat oil in 10-inch skillet over medium-high heat until hot. Cook chicken in oil 15 to 20 minutes, turning once, until juice of chicken is no longer pink when centers of thickest pieces are cut. Stir in apples and wine. Cook about 4 minutes, stirring occasionally, until apples are tender. Stir in jelly; cook and stir until jelly is melted. *4 servings.*

NUTRITION INFORMATION PER SERVING

1 serving		Percent of U.S. RDA	
Calories	295	Vitamin A	*
Protein, g	26	Vitamin C	4%
Carbohydrate, g	33	Calcium	2%
Fat, g	7	Iron	6%
Cholesterol, mg	65		
Sodium, mg	210		

Skillet Chicken Parmigiana

4 skinless boneless chicken breast halves (about 1 pound)

⅓ cup Italian-style dry bread crumbs

⅓ cup grated Parmesan cheese

1 egg, beaten

2 tablespoons olive or vegetable oil

2 cups spaghetti sauce

½ cup shredded mozzarella cheese (2 ounces)

Flatten chicken breast halves to ¼-inch thickness between plastic wrap or waxed paper. Mix bread crumbs and Parmesan cheese. Dip chicken into egg; coat with bread crumb mixture. Heat oil in 12-inch skillet over medium heat until hot. Cook chicken in oil 10 to 15 minutes, turning once, until juice of chicken is no longer pink when centers of thickest pieces are cut. Stir in spaghetti sauce. Cook over low heat 2 to 3 minutes or until sauce is hot. Sprinkle mozzarella cheese over chicken. Serve with hot cooked pasta if desired. *4 servings.*

NUTRITION INFORMATION PER SERVING

1 serving		Percent of U.S. RDA	
Calories	395	Vitamin A	12%
Protein, g	37	Vitamin C	4%
Carbohydrate, g	18	Calcium	26%
Fat, g	21	Iron	14%
Cholesterol, mg	135		
Sodium, mg	1150		

Chicken with Glazed Apples

Chicken Cilantro

2 tablespoons vegetable oil

¼ cup chopped onion (about 1 small)

1 clove garlic, finely chopped

1 pound skinless boneless chicken breasts, cut into 1-inch pieces

1 teaspoon salt

⅛ teaspoon pepper

2 tablespoons chopped fresh cilantro

Heat oil in 10-inch skillet over medium-high heat. Cook onion and garlic in oil, stirring frequently, until onion is tender. Stir in chicken, salt and pepper. Cook, stirring occasionally, until chicken is no longer pink in center. Stir in cilantro. Pour drippings over chicken to serve. *4 servings.*

NUTRITION INFORMATION PER SERVING

1 serving		*Percent of U.S. RDA*	
Calories	200	Vitamin A	*
Protein, g	25	Vitamin C	*
Carbohydrate, g	2	Calcium	2%
Fat, g	10	Iron	6%
Cholesterol, mg	60		
Sodium, mg	590		

Stuffed Turkey Tenderloins

2 turkey breast tenderloins (about 1½ pounds)

⅓ cup Italian-style dry bread crumbs

¼ cup chopped green onions (2 to 3 medium)

2 tablespoons slivered almonds

1 can (4 ounces) mushroom stems and pieces, well drained

2 tablespoons margarine or butter, melted

Horseradish Sauce (right)

Heat oven to 350°. Cut a slit in each turkey tenderloin to within ½ inch of ends, forming a pocket. Mix bread crumbs, green onions, almonds and mushrooms. Fill pockets with bread crumb mixture; secure with string or toothpicks. Place in greased square pan, 9×9×2 inches. Brush with margarine. Bake uncovered 30 to 40 minutes or until juice of turkey is no longer pink when center of thickest piece is cut. Cut turkey into slices. Serve with Horseradish Sauce. *4 servings.*

HORSERADISH SAUCE

½ cup sour cream

2 tablespoons milk

1 tablespoon prepared horseradish

¼ teaspoon salt

Mix all ingredients.

NUTRITION INFORMATION PER SERVING

1 serving		*Percent of U.S. RDA*	
Calories	390	Vitamin A	12%
Protein, g	44	Vitamin C	*
Carbohydrate, g	11	Calcium	10%
Fat, g	20	Iron	14%
Cholesterol, mg	120		
Sodium, mg	490		

Grilled Turkey Breast with Plum Sauce

4-pound boneless whole turkey breast
½ teaspoon lemon pepper
¼ cup plum jam
Plum Sauce (below)

Heat oven to 350°. Place turkey breast, skin side up, on rack in shallow roasting pan. Sprinkle with lemon pepper. Insert meat thermometer in center of turkey breast. Cover and bake 50 minutes. Uncover and bake 20 to 30 minutes longer, brushing with plum jam, until thermometer reads 170° and juice of turkey is no longer pink when center is cut. Serve turkey with Plum Sauce. *8 servings.*

PLUM SAUCE

1 cup sliced plums
¼ cup plum jam
1 tablespoon white vinegar

Mix all ingredients in 1-quart saucepan. Cook over medium heat about 5 minutes, stirring occasionally, until plums are tender.

TO GRILL: Prepare grill, arranging coals around edge of firebox. Place drip pan under grilling area. Grease cooking surface of grill. Sprinkle turkey breast with lemon pepper. Insert meat thermometer in center of turkey breast. Cover and grill turkey, skin side down, 4 to 6 inches from medium coals 30 minutes; turn turkey. Cover and grill 40 to 50 minutes longer, brushing with plum jam during last 10 minutes, until thermometer reads 170° and juice of turkey is no longer pink when center is cut.

NUTRITION INFORMATION PER SERVING

1 serving		Percent of U.S. RDA	
Calories	380	Vitamin A	2%
Protein, g	45	Vitamin C	2%
Carbohydrate, g	16	Calcium	2%
Fat, g	15	Iron	12%
Cholesterol, mg	125		
Sodium, mg	115		

Turkey with Chiles and Cheese

Canned whole green chiles are usually mild Anaheims. If you like hotter foods, try seeded split jalapeños.

1 tablespoon vegetable oil

2 turkey breast tenderloins (about 1½ pounds)

1 can (4 ounces) whole green chiles, drained

⅔ cup shredded Monterey Jack cheese

1 egg, beaten

1 cup crushed corn chips

1 cup chopped tomato (about 1 large)

Heat oven to 350°. Spread oil in square pan, 9×9×2 inches. Cut a slit in each turkey tenderloin to within ½ inch of ends, forming a pocket. Fill pockets with chiles and cheese; secure with string or toothpicks. Dip turkey into egg; coat with corn chips. Place in pan. Bake uncovered 30 to 40 minutes or until juice of turkey is no longer pink when center of thickest piece is cut. Cut turkey into slices. Serve with tomato. *4 servings.*

NUTRITION INFORMATION PER SERVING

1 serving		Percent of U.S. RDA	
Calories	370	Vitamin A	12%
Protein, g	46	Vitamin C	22%
Carbohydrate, g	7	Calcium	16%
Fat, g	18	Iron	12%
Cholesterol, mg	170		
Sodium, mg	600		

Turkey Medallions with Cranberry and Orange

If you are using fresh cranberries, cook the sauce about 10 minutes or until the cranberries pop.

¼ cup dry white wine or chicken broth

2 tablespoons orange juice

1½ pounds turkey breast tenderloins, cut into ½-inch slices

1 cup orange marmalade

½ cup dried or fresh cranberries

¼ cup orange juice

Mix wine and 2 tablespoons orange juice in shallow glass or plastic dish. Add turkey; stir to coat with marinade. Cover and refrigerate 30 minutes.

Place turkey and marinade in 10-inch skillet. Cook over medium heat 15 to 20 minutes, stirring occasionally, until turkey is no longer pink in center. Mix marmalade, cranberries and ¼ cup orange juice in 1-quart saucepan. Cook over low heat 5 minutes, stirring occasionally. Place turkey on serving platter. Top with marmalade mixture. *4 servings.*

NUTRITION INFORMATION PER SERVING

1 serving		Percent of U.S. RDA	
Calories	425	Vitamin A	*
Protein, g	40	Vitamin C	14%
Carbohydrate, g	56	Calcium	4%
Fat, g	5	Iron	12%
Cholesterol, mg	100		
Sodium, mg	130		

Turkey Medallions with Cranberry and Orange

CHAPTER
4

Drumsticks & Thighs

We all love drumsticks, and in this inventive chapter you'll learn that there are many delicious and creative ways to cook drumsticks and thighs. Of course, there are wonderful classic recipes that showcase drumsticks in all their glory, such as Glazed Chicken Drumsticks and Delicious Drumsticks. But you'll also find delightful new ideas such as Tangy Chicken Thighs with Artichokes, Sesame Chicken Stir-fry with Mushrooms and Turkey Thigh Fajitas.

You can use the special section on International Flavors to turn everyday chicken into a meal with foreign flair. Create dinners with Caribbean, Mexican, North African, Provençale or Thai flavors any night that you'd like to take a trip away from the ordinary!

Three-Herb Chicken (page 120)

Glazed Chicken Drumsticks

4 chicken drumsticks (about 1 pound)

3 tablespoons soy sauce

2 tablespoons honey

1 tablespoon vegetable oil

1 tablespoon chile sauce

¼ teaspoon ground ginger

⅛ teaspoon garlic powder

Place drumsticks in ungreased rectangular baking dish, 13×9×2 inches. Mix remaining ingredients; pour over chicken. Cover and refrigerate 4 to 6 hours.

Heat oven to 375°. Remove chicken from marinade; reserve marinade. Place chicken on rack in broiler pan. Brush with marinade. Bake uncovered 50 to 60 minutes or until juice of chicken is no longer pink when centers of thickest pieces are cut. Discard any remaining marinade. *4 servings.*

NUTRITION INFORMATION PER SERVING

1 serving		*Percent of U.S. RDA*	
Calories	195	Vitamin A	2%
Protein, g	14	Vitamin C	*
Carbohydrate, g	10	Calcium	2%
Fat, g	11	Iron	6%
Cholesterol, mg	45		
Sodium, mg	830		

Delicious Drumsticks

½ cup all-purpose flour

½ teaspoon salt

½ teaspoon paprika

¼ teaspoon pepper

6 chicken drumsticks (about 1½ pounds)

¼ cup (½ stick) margarine or butter, melted and cooled

Heat oven to 425°. Mix flour, salt, paprika and pepper. Dip drumsticks into margarine; coat with flour mixture. Arrange in ungreased square pan, 8×8×2 inches. Bake uncovered about 50 minutes or until juice of chicken is no longer pink when centers of thickest pieces are cut. *6 servings.*

NUTRITION INFORMATION PER SERVING

1 serving		*Percent of U.S. RDA*	
Calories	225	Vitamin A	12%
Protein, g	15	Vitamin C	*
Carbohydrate, g	8	Calcium	2%
Fat, g	15	Iron	8%
Cholesterol, mg	45		
Sodium, mg	310		

Tandoori Chicken Drumsticks

This easy dish has many of the same flavors as traditional tandoori chicken from India without the lengthy cooking time.

1 tablespoon vegetable oil

8 chicken drumsticks (about 2 pounds)

½ cup chopped onion (about 1 medium)

½ cup chicken broth

2 teaspoons curry powder

1 teaspoon packed brown sugar

¼ teaspoon salt

2 cloves garlic, finely chopped

1 container (8 ounces) plain yogurt

1 tablespoon all-purpose flour

Heat oil in 12-inch skillet over medium heat until hot. Cook drumsticks in oil about 15 minutes, turning occasionally, until brown on all sides; drain.

Mix onion, broth, curry powder, brown sugar, salt and garlic; add to chicken in skillet. Heat to boiling; reduce heat. Cover and simmer about 35 minutes, stirring occasionally and turning chicken once, until juice of chicken is no longer pink when centers of thickest pieces are cut.

Remove chicken from skillet, using tongs; keep warm. Mix yogurt and flour; stir into mixture in skillet. Cook and stir until thickened; continue cooking 1 minute (do not boil). Serve sauce with chicken. Serve over hot cooked rice if desired. *4 servings.*

NUTRITION INFORMATION PER SERVING

1 serving		Percent of U.S. RDA	
Calories	335	Vitamin A	4%
Protein, g	32	Vitamin C	2%
Carbohydrate, g	10	Calcium	14%
Fat, g	19	Iron	14%
Cholesterol, mg	95		
Sodium, mg	360		

Cashew Drumsticks

For a picnic treat, chill these nutty drumsticks.

1 cup ground cashews

*1½ tablespoons chopped fresh or 1½
teaspoons dried basil leaves*

1½ teaspoons chile powder

1 teaspoon ground cumin

¼ teaspoon salt

*¼ cup (½ stick) margarine or butter,
melted*

¼ teaspoon red pepper sauce

8 chicken drumsticks (about 2 pounds)

Heat oven to 425°. Grease rectangular pan,
13×9×2 inches. Mix cashews, basil, chile powder, cumin and salt. Mix margarine and pepper
sauce. Dip drumsticks into margarine mixture;
coat with cashew mixture. Bake uncovered 20
minutes; turn chicken. Bake uncovered about 20
minutes longer or until juice of chicken is no
longer pink when centers of thickest pieces are
cut. *4 servings.*

NUTRITION INFORMATION PER SERVING

1 serving		Percent of U.S. RDA	
Calories	585	Vitamin A	22%
Protein, g	35	Vitamin C	*
Carbohydrate, g	13	Calcium	6%
Fat, g	45	Iron	24%
Cholesterol, mg	95		
Sodium, mg	620		

Cashew Drumsticks

Apricot-glazed Chicken Drumsticks

**You can also use this fruity glaze to dress up
roasted chicken pieces or whole Cornish hens.**

8 chicken drumsticks (about 2 pounds)

2 tablespoons apricot preserves

2 tablespoons French dressing

2 teaspoons lemon juice

½ teaspoon ground mustard

Heat oven to 375°. Grease rack of broiler pan.
Place drumsticks on rack in broiler pan. Bake
uncovered 30 minutes.

Mix remaining ingredients; brush on chicken.
Bake uncovered about 10 minutes longer, brushing twice with apricot mixture, until juice of
chicken is no longer pink when centers of thickest
pieces are cut. *4 servings.*

TO GRILL: Cover and grill drumsticks 4 to 6
inches from medium coals 20 minutes; turn
chicken. Cover and grill 20 minutes longer. Brush
apricot mixture on chicken. Cover and grill about
10 minutes longer, brushing twice with apricot
mixture, until juice of chicken is no longer pink
when centers of thickest pieces are cut.

NUTRITION INFORMATION PER SERVING

1 serving		Percent of U.S. RDA	
Calories	305	Vitamin A	2%
Protein, g	28	Vitamin C	*
Carbohydrate, g	8	Calcium	2%
Fat, g	18	Iron	10%
Cholesterol, mg	100		
Sodium, mg	200		

Orange-Pineapple Chicken with Walnuts

1 tablespoon vegetable oil

8 chicken drumsticks (about 2 pounds)

1 can (15¼ ounces) pineapple tidbits, undrained

¾ cup orange juice

1 medium onion, cut into thin wedges

⅓ cup currants or raisins

¼ cup rum or orange juice

1 teaspoon ground coriander

½ teaspoon ground allspice

¼ teaspoon salt

⅛ teaspoon pepper

3 tablespoons cold water

1 tablespoon plus 1 teaspoon cornstarch

1 cup coarsely chopped tomato (about 1 medium)

⅓ cup chopped walnuts

Heat oil in 12-inch skillet over medium heat until hot. Cook drumsticks in oil about 15 minutes, turning occasionally, until brown on all sides; remove from skillet. Drain drippings from skillet.

Mix pineapple, orange juice, onion, currants, rum, coriander, allspice, salt and pepper in skillet. Return chicken to skillet. Heat to boiling; reduce heat. Cover and simmer 30 to 35 minutes, stirring occasionally, until juice of chicken is no longer pink when centers of thickest pieces are cut.

Remove chicken from skillet, using tongs; keep warm. Mix water and cornstarch; stir into mixture in skillet. Heat to boiling, stirring constantly. Boil and stir 1 minute. Stir in tomato and walnuts; heat through. Serve sauce with chicken. Serve over hot cooked brown rice if desired. *4 servings.*

NUTRITION INFORMATION PER SERVING

1 serving		*Percent of U.S. RDA*	
Calories	475	Vitamin A	6%
Protein, g	31	Vitamin C	28%
Carbohydrate, g	37	Calcium	6%
Fat, g	24	Iron	18%
Cholesterol, mg	95		
Sodium, mg	230		

Creamy Mulligatawny Soup

This creamy curried soup is based on the spicy Indian classic.

1 medium all-purpose apple, sliced

2 cups chicken broth

1 cup sliced carrots (about 2 medium)

1 cup chopped onion (about 1 large)

1 cup apple juice

1 tablespoon lemon juice

2 teaspoons curry powder

½ teaspoon ground allspice

¼ teaspoon pepper

6 chicken drumsticks (about 1½ pounds), skinned

1 cup milk

⅓ cup all-purpose flour

1 cup coarsely chopped tomato (about 1 medium)

Chopped fresh cilantro, if desired

Mix apple, broth, carrots, onion, apple juice, lemon juice, curry powder, allspice and pepper in Dutch oven. Add drumsticks. Heat to boiling; reduce heat. Cover and simmer about 40 minutes, stirring occasionally, until juice of chicken is no longer pink when centers of thickest pieces are cut.

Remove chicken from Dutch oven; cut chicken meat from bones. Return chicken meat to Dutch oven.

Shake milk and flour in tightly covered container until smooth; gradually stir into chicken mixture. Heat to boiling, stirring constantly. Boil and stir 1 minute. Stir in tomato; heat through. Serve over hot cooked rice in shallow soup bowls if desired. Sprinkle with cilantro. *4 servings.*

NUTRITION INFORMATION PER SERVING

1 serving		*Percent of U.S. RDA*	
Calories	340	Vitamin A	88%
Protein, g	27	Vitamin C	10%
Carbohydrate, g	33	Calcium	12%
Fat, g	13	Iron	18%
Cholesterol, mg	75		
Sodium, mg	510		

Cheese-stuffed Chicken Drumsticks

⅓ cup shredded Swiss cheese

3 tablespoons grated Romano or Parmesan cheese

1 tablespoon dry bread crumbs

1½ teaspoons Italian seasoning

¼ teaspoon pepper

1 package (3 ounces) cream cheese, softened

8 chicken drumsticks (about 2 pounds)

1 tablespoon margarine or butter, melted

Heat oven to 375°. Grease rack of broiler pan. Mix all ingredients except drumsticks and margarine.

Beginning at wide end of drumstick, carefully separate skin from chicken, leaving skin attached at narrow end of bone. Fill opening with about 1 tablespoon cheese mixture. Place chicken on rack in broiler pan. Brush with margarine. Bake uncovered about 50 minutes or until juice of chicken is no longer pink when centers of thickest pieces are cut. *4 servings.*

NUTRITION INFORMATION PER SERVING

1 serving		*Percent of U.S. RDA*	
Calories	410	Vitamin A	16%
Protein, g	34	Vitamin C	*
Carbohydrate, g	3	Calcium	20%
Fat, g	29	Iron	14%
Cholesterol, mg	130		
Sodium, mg	290		

Spicy Cancún Drumsticks

⅓ cup all-purpose flour

⅓ cup yellow cornmeal

1 teaspoon chopped fresh or ¼ teaspoon dried oregano leaves

1 teaspoon chopped fresh or ¼ teaspoon dried basil leaves

½ teaspoon ground cumin

½ teaspoon chile powder

¼ teaspoon salt

⅛ teaspoon ground cloves

⅓ cup buttermilk

¼ teaspoon red pepper sauce

8 chicken drumsticks (about 2 pounds), skinned

Heat oven to 400°. Grease rectangular pan, 13×9×2 inches. Mix all ingredients except buttermilk, pepper sauce and chicken drumsticks in large plastic bag. Mix buttermilk and pepper sauce. Dip chicken into buttermilk mixture; shake in bag to coat with cornmeal mixture. Place in pan. Bake uncovered 40 to 45 minutes or until juice is no longer pink when centers of thickest pieces are cut. *4 servings.*

NUTRITION INFORMATION PER SERVING

1 serving		*Percent of U.S. RDA*	
Calories	230	Vitamin A	2%
Protein, g	30	Vitamin C	*
Carbohydrate, g	18	Calcium	4%
Fat, g	4	Iron	12%
Cholesterol, mg	70		
Sodium, mg	230		

Cheese-stuffed Chicken Drumsticks

Chicken Drumsticks in Red Wine

2 slices bacon, cut into 1-inch pieces

8 chicken drumsticks (about 2 pounds)

1½ cups small fresh whole mushrooms

1½ cups whole baby-cut carrots

1 cup sliced leeks

1⅓ cups dry red wine or chicken broth

2 teaspoons Italian seasoning

½ teaspoon salt

¼ teaspoon pepper

2 cloves garlic, finely chopped

1 bay leaf

1 package (9 ounces) frozen artichoke hearts, thawed

3 tablespoons cold water

1 tablespoon plus 1 teaspoon cornstarch

Cook bacon in 12-inch skillet over medium heat, stirring occasionally, until crisp. Remove bacon from skillet, using slotted spoon; drain on paper towels. Drain all but 1 tablespoon bacon fat from skillet. Cook drumsticks in bacon fat over medium heat about 15 minutes, turning occasionally, until brown on all sides; drain.

Add remaining ingredients except water and cornstarch to chicken in skillet. Heat to boiling; reduce heat. Cover and simmer 30 to 40 minutes, stirring occasionally, until juice of chicken is no longer pink when centers of thickest pieces are cut. Remove chicken from skillet, using tongs; keep warm. Discard bay leaf.

Skim fat from liquid in skillet. Mix water and cornstarch; stir into mixture in skillet. Heat to boiling, stirring constantly. Boil and stir 1 minute. Stir in bacon. Serve sauce with chicken. Serve over hot cooked noodles if desired. *4 servings.*

NUTRITION INFORMATION PER SERVING

1 serving		Percent of U.S. RDA	
Calories	345	Vitamin A	100%
Protein, g	33	Vitamin C	12%
Carbohydrate, g	22	Calcium	10%
Fat, g	16	Iron	26%
Cholesterol, mg	95		
Sodium, mg	520		

Five-Spice Chicken

Using a broiler rack and pan helps keep the chicken out of the baking juices so it stays crispy.

1 tablespoon sesame or vegetable oil

1 teaspoon paprika

1 teaspoon five-spice powder

4 chicken thigh-and-drumstick hindquarters (about 3 pounds)

1/4 cup apricot preserves

1 tablespoon soy sauce

1/2 teaspoon grated orange peel

Heat oven to 375°. Grease rack of broiler pan. Mix oil, paprika and five-spice powder. Rub hindquarters with oil mixture. Place chicken on rack in broiler pan. Bake uncovered 40 minutes.

Mix remaining ingredients; brush on chicken. Bake uncovered about 10 minutes longer, brushing once with preserves mixture, until juice of chicken is no longer pink when centers of thickest pieces are cut. *4 servings.*

NUTRITION INFORMATION PER SERVING

1 serving		*Percent of U.S. RDA*	
Calories	350	Vitamin A	6%
Protein, g	31	Vitamin C	2%
Carbohydrate, g	14	Calcium	2%
Fat, g	19	Iron	12%
Cholesterol, mg	105		
Sodium, mg	360		

Caribbean Chicken

4 chicken drumsticks (about 1 pound)

4 chicken thighs (about 1 pound)

2 cans (15 ounces each) black beans, rinsed and drained

2 green onions, thinly sliced

1 clove garlic, finely chopped

1 cup cubed mango or 1 can (8 ounces) sliced peaches, drained and cut up

1 tablespoon grated gingerroot or 1 teaspoon ground ginger

2 tablespoons lime juice

1 teaspoon grated lime peel

1/2 teaspoon salt

Hot cooked rice, if desired

Heat oven to 375°. Place chicken pieces, skin sides up, in ungreased rectangular baking dish, 13×9×2 inches. Bake uncovered 40 minutes. Drain drippings.

Mix remaining ingredients except rice. Spoon over and around chicken pieces. Cover and bake about 30 minutes or until juice of chicken is no longer pink when centers of thickest pieces are cut. Serve with rice. *4 servings.*

NUTRITION INFORMATION PER SERVING

1 serving		*Percent of U.S. RDA*	
Calories	525	Vitamin A	20%
Protein, g	44	Vitamin C	12%
Carbohydrate, g	49	Calcium	14%
Fat, g	17	Iron	34%
Cholesterol, mg	100		
Sodium, mg	730		

International Flavors

The saying "Variety is the spice of life" certainly is true when exploring the many different ethnic or international flavors of the world. Herbs and spices, along with other indigenous ingredients, help give various countries and regions within their borders very distinctive flavors.

The international flavors that follow offer a culinary tour of some of the most popular ethnic cuisines and let you create their special flavors at home. Our enticing tour will bring the flavors of the Caribbean, Mexico, North Africa, Provence (France) and Thailand into your kitchen with recipes for a basic seasoning mix and additional recipes that use the mix. Now, without traveling, you can sit back in the comfort of your home and enjoy some of the world's most flavorful cuisines!

Cooking Directions:

Choose a flavor and the cooking method to match from the chart below and prepare your dish using 4 skinless boneless chicken breast halves or thighs (about 1 pound).

Rub: Heat oven to 375°. Brush chicken with oil and rub with seasoning mix (see individual recipes below). Place chicken in greased square baking pan, 9×9×2 inches. Bake for 35 to 45 minutes, turning once, until juice of chicken is no longer pink when centers of thickest pieces are cut.

Marinade: Prepare marinade as directed below. Combine chicken and marinade in a sealable, heavy-duty plastic freezer bag. Refrigerate 1 to 2 hours.

- To Broil: Place chicken on rack in broiler pan. Broil 4 to 6 inches from heat 15 to 20 minutes, turning once and brushing frequently with marinade, until juice of chicken is no longer pink when centers of thickest pieces are cut. Discard any remaining marinade.

- To Grill: Grill chicken 4 to 6 inches from medium coals 15 to 20 minutes, turning once, until juice of chicken is no longer pink when centers of thickest pieces are cut.

Sauté: Heat oil in 12-inch skillet over medium-high heat until hot; add chicken and seasoning mix (see individual recipes at right). Cook chicken until browned, about 2 minutes per side. Add remaining ingredients. Reduce heat; cover and simmer 10 to 15 minutes or until juice of chicken is no longer pink when centers of thickest pieces are cut.

Special Note for Thai Sauté:

- Do not add peanuts with remaining ingredients. Sprinkle chicken mixture with peanuts just before serving.

Serving Suggestions for Sauté Recipes:

- Caribbean: cooked rice

- Mexican: flour tortillas

- North African: cooked couscous

- Provençale: crusty French bread

- Thai: cooked Chinese wheat noodles

CARIBBEAN FLAVORS

Caribbean Seasoning Mix

⅓ cup instant minced onion

1 tablespoon dry mustard

2 teaspoons ground allspice

2 teaspoons ground cinnamon

2 teaspoons crushed red pepper

1 teaspoon garlic powder

½ teaspoon salt

Mix together in storage container with tight-fitting lid. Store in cool, dry location for up to 6 months. Shake or stir to combine before each use. About ½ cup mix.

Caribbean Rub

1 tablespoon vegetable oil

2 tablespoons Caribbean Seasoning Mix

Caribbean Marinade

½ cup pineapple juice

2 tablespoons Caribbean Seasoning Mix

1 tablespoon grated orange peel

1 tablespoon vegetable oil

Caribbean Sauté

1 tablespoon vegetable oil

¼ cup Caribbean Seasoning Mix

1 small yellow or red bell pepper, sliced

1 small red onion, sliced

1 papaya, peeled, seeded and sliced

MEXICAN FLAVORS

Mexican Seasoning Mix

¼ cup ground red chiles or chile powder

3 tablespoons dried oregano leaves

1 tablespoon ground cumin

2 teaspoons ground coriander

½ teaspoon salt

Mix together in storage container with tight-fitting lid. Store in cool, dry location for up to 6 months. Shake or stir to combine before each use. About ½ cup mix.

Mexican Rub

1 tablespoon vegetable oil

2 tablespoons Mexican Seasoning Mix

Mexican Marinade

¼ cup dry white wine or chicken broth

¼ cup lime juice

2 tablespoons Mexican Seasoning Mix

1 tablespoon vegetable oil

Mexican Sauté

1 tablespoon oil

¼ cup Mexican Seasoning Mix

¼ cup pumpkin or sunflower seeds

2 medium tomatoes, chopped

2 poblano chiles, chopped, or 1 small green bell pepper, chopped

1 can (11 ounces) tomatillos, drained

(Recipes continue on following pages)

NORTH AFRICAN FLAVORS

North African Seasoning Mix

½ *cup chopped fresh cilantro*

¼ *cup chopped fresh mint*

1 tablespoon paprika

¾ *teaspoon salt*

½ *teaspoon saffron threads, crushed, or*
  ground turmeric

Mix together in storage container with tight-fitting lid. Refrigerate up to 5 days. Stir to combine before each use. About ½ cup mix.

North African Rub

1 tablespoon olive oil

2 tablespoons North African Seasoning Mix

North African Marinade

¼ *cup lemon juice*

¼ *cup olive oil*

2 tablespoons North African Seasoning Mix

2 garlic cloves, finely chopped

North African Sauté

1 tablespoon olive oil

¼ *cup North African Seasoning Mix*

1 cup whole dates

½ *cup chicken broth*

1 small lemon, cut into thin wedges

1 can (15 to 16 ounces) garbanzo beans,
  drained

PROVENÇALE FLAVORS

Provençale Seasoning Mix

¼ *cup dried tarragon leaves*

3 tablespoons dried thyme leaves

2 tablespoons dried sage leaves, crumbled

2 teaspoons onion powder

¾ *teaspoon salt*

Mix together in storage container with tight-fitting lid. Store in cool, dry location for up to 6 months. Shake or stir to combine before each use. About ½ cup mix.

Provençale Rub

1 tablespoon olive oil

2 tablespoons Provençale Seasoning Mix

Provençale Marinade

½ *cup dry red wine or chicken broth*

2 tablespoons Provençale Seasoning Mix

1 tablespoon olive oil

1 clove garlic, finely chopped

Provençale Sauté

1 tablespoon olive oil

¼ *cup Provençale Seasoning Mix*

8 ounces fresh mushrooms, halved

5 shallots, peeled, halved

1 medium tomato, seeded, chopped

1 package (10 ounces) frozen artichoke hearts,
  thawed and halved

THAI FLAVORS

Thai Seasoning Mix

⅓ cup chopped fresh lemongrass

3 tablespoons grated lemonpeel

1 tablespoon Chinese five-spice powder

¾ teaspoon salt

½ teaspoon garlic powder

Mix together in storage container with tight-fitting lid. Store in refrigerator for up to 1 week. Stir to combine before each use. About ½ cup mix.

Thai Rub

1 tablespoon vegetable oil

2 tablespoons Thai Seasoning Mix

Thai Marinade

2 tablespoons Thai Seasoning Mix

1 tablespoon vegetable oil

Thai Sauté

1 tablespoon vegetable oil

¼ cup Thai Seasoning Mix

¼ cup sliced green onions

¼ chopped dry roasted peanuts

2 jalapeño chiles, seeded and chopped

1 can (15 ounces) lychees, drained

Three-Herb Chicken

This is a great recipe for busy weekend days. Just combine the chicken and marinade ingredients in the morning and let them chill in the refrigerator all day. When dinnertime rolls around, pop the chicken in the oven. Because there's little last-minute preparation, you can put your feet up and relax while the chicken bakes.

½ cup vegetable oil

½ cup lime juice

2 tablespoons chopped fresh or 2 teaspoons dried basil leaves

2 tablespoons chopped fresh or 2 teaspoons dried chervil leaves

2 tablespoons chopped fresh or 2 teaspoons dried thyme leaves

1 teaspoon onion powder

¼ teaspoon lemon pepper

4 chicken thigh-and-drumstick hindquarters (about 3 pounds)

Mix all ingredients except chicken hindquarters in sealable heavy-duty plastic bag or glass bowl. Add hindquarters; turn to coat with marinade. Seal bag or cover dish; refrigerate at least 3 to 4 hours, turning occasionally.

Heat oven to 375°. Grease rack of broiler pan. Remove chicken from marinade; reserve marinade. Place chicken on rack in broiler pan. Bake uncovered 30 minutes; turn chicken. Brush with marinade. Bake uncovered about 45 minutes longer or until juice of chicken is no longer pink when centers of thickest pieces are cut. Discard any remaining marinade. *4 servings.*

NUTRITION INFORMATION PER SERVING

1 serving		*Percent of U.S. RDA*	
Calories	390	Vitamin A	4%
Protein, g	30	Vitamin C	2%
Carbohydrate, g	2	Calcium	4%
Fat, g	29	Iron	14%
Cholesterol, mg	105		
Sodium, mg	95		

Chicken Smothered with Peppers

For a very pretty dish, try using two different colors of bell peppers, such as red and yellow.

1 tablespoon vegetable oil

8 chicken thighs (about 2 pounds)

2 cloves garlic, finely chopped

1 cup mushroom halves

⅓ cup sliced pimiento-stuffed olives

¼ cup dry sherry or chicken broth

1½ tablespoons chopped fresh or 1½ teaspoons dried marjoram leaves

1 tablespoon chopped fresh or 1 teaspoon dried oregano leaves

½ teaspoon salt

¼ teaspoon pepper

2 large red, yellow or green bell peppers, cut into ¼-inch strips

1 medium onion, sliced

2 tablespoons cold water

1 tablespoon cornstarch

Heat oil in 10-inch skillet over medium heat until hot. Cook thighs and garlic in oil about 10 minutes, turning chicken once and stirring garlic occasionally, until chicken is brown; drain.

Add remaining ingredients except water and cornstarch to chicken in skillet. Heat to boiling; reduce heat. Cover and simmer 30 to 40 minutes, stirring vegetable mixture occasionally, until juice of chicken is no longer pink when centers of thickest pieces are cut. Remove chicken from skillet, using tongs; keep warm. Mix water and cornstarch; stir into mixture in skillet. Heat to boiling, stirring constantly. Boil and stir about 1 minute or until thickened. Serve vegetable mixture over chicken. *4 servings.*

NUTRITION INFORMATION PER SERVING

1 serving		Percent of U.S. RDA	
Calories	370	Vitamin A	32%
Protein, g	34	Vitamin C	82%
Carbohydrate, g	11	Calcium	6%
Fat, g	22	Iron	18%
Cholesterol, mg	110		
Sodium, mg	640		

Paella Casserole

Rosamarina is a tiny, rice-shaped pasta that's also called orzo.

1 package (9 ounces) frozen artichoke
   hearts, thawed

1 tablespoon olive or vegetable oil

4 skinless boneless chicken thighs (about
   ¾ pound)

½ cup chopped onion (about 1 medium)

3 cloves garlic, finely chopped

1 cup uncooked rosamarina (orzo) pasta

1 cup chicken broth

¾ teaspoon ground turmeric

¼ teaspoon ground red pepper (cayenne)

4 ounces frozen cooked shrimp, thawed

1 can (14½ ounces) stewed tomatoes,
   undrained

1 can (6½ ounces) minced clams,
   undrained

Heat oven to 350°. Cut any large artichoke hearts in half. Heat oil in 10-inch skillet over medium heat until hot. Cook thighs in oil about 6 minutes, turning once, until brown. Remove chicken from skillet, using tongs.

Cook onion and garlic in drippings in skillet over medium-high heat about 1 minute, stirring occasionally, until onion is crisp-tender. Stir in artichoke hearts and remaining ingredients. Heat to boiling. Pour pasta mixture into ungreased rectangular baking dish, 11×7×1½ inches. Place chicken on top.

Cover and bake about 45 minutes or until juice of chicken is no longer pink when centers of thickest pieces are cut and pasta is tender. Let stand covered 5 minutes before serving. *4 servings.*

NUTRITION INFORMATION PER SERVING

1 serving		Percent of U.S. RDA	
Calories	400	Vitamin A	16%
Protein, g	40	Vitamin C	28%
Carbohydrate, g	43	Calcium	14%
Fat, g	10	Iron	98%
Cholesterol, mg	120		
Sodium, mg	570		

Herbed Chicken Thighs with Vegetables

1 tablespoon vegetable oil

8 chicken thighs, skinned (about 2 pounds)

1½ cups julienne strips carrots (about 3 medium)

1 cup frozen small whole onions

⅓ cup pitted ripe olives, cut in half

1 cup chicken broth

1½ tablespoons chopped fresh or 1½ teaspoons dried basil leaves

1 tablespoon chopped fresh or 1 teaspoon dried oregano leaves

2 tablespoons lemon juice

2 teaspoons chopped fresh or ½ teaspoon dried thyme leaves

¼ teaspoon salt

¼ teaspoon pepper

¼ cup cold water

2 tablespoons cornstarch

2 cups chopped tomatoes (about 2 large)

Heat oil in 10-inch skillet over medium heat until hot. Cook thighs in oil about 6 minutes, turning once, until brown; drain. Add remaining ingredients except water, cornstarch and tomatoes to chicken in skillet. Heat to boiling; reduce heat. Cover and simmer 30 to 40 minutes, stirring vegetable mixture occasionally, until juice of chicken is no longer pink when centers of thickest pieces are cut. Remove chicken from skillet, using tongs; keep warm.

Skim fat from liquid in skillet. Mix water and cornstarch; stir into mixture in skillet. Heat to boiling, stirring constantly. Boil and stir 1 minute. Stir in tomatoes; heat through. Serve sauce over chicken. *4 servings.*

NUTRITION INFORMATION PER SERVING

1 serving		Percent of U.S. RDA	
Calories	400	Vitamin A	92%
Protein, g	36	Vitamin C	16%
Carbohydrate, g	17	Calcium	8%
Fat, g	22	Iron	22%
Cholesterol, mg	110		
Sodium, mg	550		

Honey-Mustard Chicken Thigh Sandwiches

You can use this zesty sauce with burgers, too.

1 tablespoon vegetable oil

4 skinless boneless chicken thighs (about ¾ pound)

3 tablespoons mayonnaise or salad dressing

1 tablespoon honey

1½ teaspoons spicy brown mustard

¼ teaspoon ground ginger

⅛ teaspoon ground red pepper (cayenne)

4 hamburger buns, split and toasted

4 lettuce leaves

Heat oil in 10-inch skillet over medium heat until hot. Cook thighs in oil 10 to 12 minutes, turning once, until juice of chicken is no longer pink when centers of thickest pieces are cut. Mix remaining ingredients except buns and lettuce; spread on cut sides of buns. Fill buns with chicken and lettuce. *4 servings.*

NUTRITION INFORMATION PER SERVING

1 serving		Percent of U.S. RDA	
Calories	340	Vitamin A	4%
Protein, g	18	Vitamin C	2%
Carbohydrate, g	28	Calcium	8%
Fat, g	18	Iron	12%
Cholesterol, mg	55		
Sodium, mg	350		

Parmesan Chicken Thigh Sandwiches

Parmesan Chicken Thigh Sandwiches

4 skinless boneless chicken thighs (about ¾ pound)

1 egg, beaten

1 tablespoon water

⅓ cup Italian-style or seasoned dry bread crumbs

2 tablespoons grated Parmesan cheese

1 tablespoon olive or vegetable oil

¼ cup shredded mozzarella cheese (1 ounce)

¼ cup spaghetti sauce or pizza sauce

8 slices (½-inch thick) French or Italian bread, toasted

Flatten chicken thighs to about ¼-inch thickness between waxed paper or plastic wrap. Mix egg and water. Mix bread crumbs and Parmesan cheese. Dip chicken into egg mixture; coat with bread crumb mixture.

Heat oil in 10-inch skillet over medium heat until hot. Cook chicken in oil about 12 minutes, turning once, until juice of chicken is no longer pink when centers of thickest pieces are cut. (Add additional oil during cooking, if necessary.) Remove skillet from heat.

Sprinkle mozzarella cheese over chicken; let stand 1 minute. Spoon spaghetti sauce over cheese. Serve chicken on buns. *4 servings.*

NUTRITION INFORMATION PER SERVING

1 serving		Percent of U.S. RDA	
Calories	335	Vitamin A	4%
Protein, g	23	Vitamin C	*
Carbohydrate, g	31	Calcium	18%
Fat, g	14	Iron	14%
Cholesterol, mg	105		
Sodium, mg	520		

Chicken-Barley Stew with Cheddar Dumplings

6 skinless boneless chicken thighs (about 1 pound), cut into 1-inch pieces

1 can (14½ ounces) whole tomatoes, undrained

1 cup sliced carrots (about 2 medium)

1 cup chopped onion (about 1 large) or sliced leeks

½ cup uncooked quick-cooking barley

3½ cups chicken broth

1½ tablespoons chopped fresh or 1½ teaspoons dried basil leaves

1 tablespoon chopped fresh or 1 teaspoon dried sage leaves

¼ teaspoon pepper

2 bay leaves

Cheddar Dumplings (right)

½ cup cold water

3 tablespoons all-purpose flour

2 cups sliced zucchini (about 1 medium)

Mix chicken, tomatoes, carrots, onion, barley, broth, basil, sage, pepper and bay leaves in Dutch oven; break up tomatoes. Heat to boiling; reduce heat. Cover and simmer about 40 minutes, stirring occasionally, until chicken is no longer pink in center. Discard bay leaves.

Prepare Cheddar Dumplings. Shake water and flour in tightly covered container until smooth; gradually stir into chicken mixture. Heat to boiling, stirring constantly. Boil and stir 1 minute. Stir in zucchini. Heat to boiling. Drop dumpling dough by 6 spoonfuls onto chicken or vegetables in stew (do not drop directly into liquid). Cover and cook over medium-low heat about 10 minutes. *6 servings.*

CHEDDAR DUMPLINGS

¾ cup all-purpose flour

⅔ cup shredded sharp Cheddar cheese

1½ teaspoons baking powder

⅛ teaspoon salt

⅛ teaspoon ground red pepper (cayenne)

1 egg, beaten

¼ cup chicken broth

1 tablespoon vegetable oil

Mix flour, cheese, baking powder, salt and red pepper in small bowl. Mix egg, broth and oil; stir into flour mixture just until dry ingredients are moistened.

NUTRITION INFORMATION PER SERVING

1 serving		*Percent of U.S. RDA*	
Calories	355	Vitamin A	46%
Protein, g	27	Vitamin C	14%
Carbohydrate, g	38	Calcium	20%
Fat, g	13	Iron	20%
Cholesterol, mg	95		
Sodium, mg	880		

Chicken-Barley Stew with Cheddar Dumplings

Tangy Chicken Thighs with Artichokes

1 package (9 ounces) frozen artichoke hearts, thawed

1 tablespoon vegetable oil

6 skinless boneless chicken thighs (about 1 pound), cut into bite-size pieces

1 cup thin diagonal slices carrots (about 2 medium)

1¼ cups chicken broth

⅓ cup chopped dehydrated sun-dried tomatoes

1½ tablespoons chopped fresh or 1½ teaspoons dried savory leaves

1½ teaspoons onion powder

¼ teaspoon pepper

1 container (8 ounces) sour cream

1 tablespoon all-purpose flour

8 ounces hot cooked fettuccine or linguine

Cut any large artichoke hearts in half. Heat oil in 10-inch skillet over medium-high heat until hot. Cook chicken and carrots in oil about 3 minutes, stirring constantly, until chicken is brown. Add artichoke hearts, broth, tomatoes, savory, onion powder and pepper to chicken in skillet. Heat to boiling; reduce heat. Cover and simmer about 10 minutes, stirring occasionally, until chicken is no longer pink in center.

Mix sour cream and flour; stir into chicken mixture. Cook, stirring constantly, until thickened; continue cooking 1 minute, stirring constantly (do not boil). Serve over fettuccine. *4 servings.*

NUTRITION INFORMATION PER SERVING

1 serving		*Percent of U.S. RDA*	
Calories	545	Vitamin A	68%
Protein, g	35	Vitamin C	14%
Carbohydrate, g	54	Calcium	14%
Fat, g	24	Iron	28%
Cholesterol, mg	155		
Sodium, mg	660		

Lemon Butter–stuffed Chicken Thighs

½ cup (1 stick) margarine or butter, slightly softened

2 tablespoons finely chopped green onion

1 tablespoon chopped fresh or 1 teaspoon dried rosemary leaves

1 teaspoon lemon juice

½ teaspoon crushed red pepper

½ teaspoon grated lemon peel

8 chicken thighs (about 2 pounds)

Heat oven to 375°. Grease rack of broiler pan. Mix all ingredients except thighs. Carefully separate skin from chicken all around each thigh, leaving skin attached in one place. Fill opening with margarine mixture. Place chicken on rack in broiler pan. Bake uncovered about 50 minutes or until juice of chicken is no longer pink when centers of thickest pieces are cut. *4 servings.*

NUTRITION INFORMATION PER SERVING

1 serving		Percent of U.S. RDA	
Calories	495	Vitamin A	36%
Protein, g	33	Vitamin C	*
Carbohydrate, g	1	Calcium	4%
Fat, g	40	Iron	12%
Cholesterol, mg	110		
Sodium, mg	370		

Shortcut Brunswick Stew

6 skinless boneless chicken thighs (about 1 pound), cut into 1-inch pieces

1 cup cubed potato (about 1 medium)

2½ cups chicken broth

1½ tablespoons chopped fresh or 1½ teaspoons dried basil leaves

1 tablespoon chopped fresh or 1 teaspoon dried marjoram leaves

2 teaspoons onion powder

¼ teaspoon pepper

1 can (14½ ounces) stewed tomatoes, undrained

1 package (10 ounces) frozen mixed vegetables, thawed

Heat all ingredients to boiling in 3-quart saucepan; reduce heat. Cover and simmer about 15 minutes, stirring occasionally, until chicken is no longer pink in center and vegetables are tender. *4 servings.*

NUTRITION INFORMATION PER SERVING

1 serving		Percent of U.S. RDA	
Calories	320	Vitamin A	38%
Protein, g	31	Vitamin C	16%
Carbohydrate, g	23	Calcium	8%
Fat, g	14	Iron	20%
Cholesterol, mg	85		
Sodium, mg	750		

Sesame Chicken Stir-fry with Mushrooms

Sesame oil gives this stir-fry a rich, nutty flavor.

¾ cup chicken broth

1 tablespoon cornstarch

3 tablespoons hoisin sauce

2 tablespoons soy sauce

1 tablespoon lemon juice

1 teaspoon sesame oil

1 tablespoon vegetable oil

6 skinless boneless chicken thighs (about 1 pound), cut into bite-size pieces

2 cloves garlic, finely chopped

2 teaspoons vegetable oil

1 medium yellow summer squash, cut lengthwise in half and sliced (about 2 cups)

2 cups mushroom halves (about 8 ounces)

1½ cups Chinese pea pods

1 small onion, cut into thin wedges

Hot cooked Oriental noodles or rice

Mix broth, cornstarch, hoisin sauce, soy sauce, lemon juice and sesame oil. Heat wok or 12-inch skillet over medium-high heat until hot. Add 1 tablespoon vegetable oil; rotate wok to coat side. Add chicken and garlic; stir-fry about 5 minutes or until chicken is no longer pink in center. Remove chicken from wok.

Add 2 teaspoons vegetable oil to wok; rotate wok to coat side. Add vegetables; stir-fry 7 to 9 minutes or until crisp-tender. Stir in hoisin sauce mixture. Cook and stir about 1 minute or until thickened. Stir in chicken; heat through. Serve over noodles. Sprinkle with toasted sesame seed if desired. *4 servings.*

NUTRITION INFORMATION PER SERVING

1 serving		*Percent of U.S. RDA*	
Calories	470	Vitamin A	4%
Protein, g	31	Vitamin C	28%
Carbohydrate, g	56	Calcium	8%
Fat, g	15	Iron	28%
Cholesterol, mg	70		
Sodium, mg	1420		

Sesame Chicken Stir-fry with Mushrooms

Sichuan Pepper Chicken Stir-fry

1 tablespoon vegetable oil

1 teaspoon whole Sichuan peppercorns or whole black peppercorns, crushed

2 dried red chile peppers or ¼ teaspoon crushed red pepper

6 skinless boneless chicken thighs (about 1 pound), cut into bite-size pieces

2 teaspoons vegetable oil

1 package (16 ounces) frozen mixed broccoli, green beans, onions, mushrooms and red pepper, thawed

1 can (8 ounces) sliced water chestnuts, drained

⅔ cup stir-fry sauce

Heat wok or 12-inch skillet over medium-high heat until hot. Add 1 tablespoon oil; rotate wok to coat side. Add peppercorns and chile peppers; stir-fry 1 minute. Add chicken; stir-fry 4 to 6 minutes or until chicken is no longer pink in center. Remove chicken mixture from wok.

Add 2 teaspoons oil to wok; rotate wok to coat side. Add mixed vegetables and water chestnuts; stir-fry about 5 minutes or until vegetables are crisp-tender. Stir in chicken mixture and stir-fry sauce. Heat until bubbly. Remove chile peppers. *4 servings.*

NUTRITION INFORMATION PER SERVING

1 serving		Percent of U.S. RDA	
Calories	290	Vitamin A	90%
Protein, g	27	Vitamin C	28%
Carbohydrate, g	21	Calcium	8%
Fat, g	13	Iron	18%
Cholesterol, mg	70		
Sodium, mg	1500		

Turkey Drumsticks with Spicy Barbecue Sauce

4 turkey drumsticks (about 2½ pounds)

¼ teaspoon salt

¾ cup water

½ cup ketchup

½ cup chopped seeded peeled tomato (about 1 small)

¼ cup chopped green bell pepper

2 tablespoons chopped onion

1 tablespoon packed brown sugar

1 teaspoon instant coffee crystals

½ teaspoon Worcestershire sauce

¼ teaspoon garlic powder

¼ teaspoon ground cinnamon

¼ teaspoon ground ginger

Grease rectangular baking dish, 11×7×1½ inches. Place drumsticks in 10-inch skillet; sprinkle with salt. Add water. Heat to boiling; reduce heat. Cover and simmer about 1 hour, turning turkey occasionally, until juice of turkey is no longer pink when centers of thickest pieces are cut. (Add additional water during cooking, if necessary.) Remove turkey from skillet to baking dish.

Heat oven to 350°. Mix remaining ingredients in 1-quart saucepan. Heat to boiling; reduce heat. Cover and simmer about 5 minutes, stirring occasionally, until bell pepper is crisp-tender. Spoon some of the sauce over turkey. Bake uncovered 15 minutes, brushing occasionally with sauce. Serve turkey with remaining sauce. *4 servings.*

NUTRITION INFORMATION PER SERVING

1 serving		Percent of U.S. RDA	
Calories	450	Vitamin A	6%
Protein, g	59	Vitamin C	10%
Carbohydrate, g	10	Calcium	4%
Fat, g	20	Iron	16%
Cholesterol, mg	165		
Sodium, mg	460		

hours or until juice of turkey is no longer pink when centers of thickest pieces are cut.

Heat 1 teaspoon oil in 1-quart saucepan over medium heat until hot. Cook onion in oil about 3 minutes, stirring frequently, until crisp-tender. Stir in remaining ingredients except water and cornstarch. Mix water and cornstarch; stir into corn mixture. Heat to boiling, stirring constantly. Boil and stir about 1 minute or until thickened. Serve sauce over turkey. *4 servings.*

NUTRITION INFORMATION PER SERVING

1 serving		Percent of U.S. RDA	
Calories	490	Vitamin A	20%
Protein, g	60	Vitamin C	28%
Carbohydrate, g	9	Calcium	4%
Fat, g	24	Iron	16%
Cholesterol, mg	165		
Sodium, mg	290		

Baked Turkey Drumsticks with Mexican Vegetable Sauce

This sauce is also wonderful with baked chicken or roast pork.

> *4 turkey drumsticks (about 2½ pounds)*
>
> *1 tablespoon vegetable oil*
>
> *1 teaspoon vegetable oil*
>
> *¼ cup chopped onion (about 1 small)*
>
> *½ cup frozen whole kernel corn*
>
> *2 teaspoons chopped fresh or ½ teaspoon dried cilantro leaves*
>
> *2 teaspoons chopped fresh or ½ teaspoon dried oregano leaves*
>
> *¼ teaspoon sugar*
>
> *1 can (5½ ounces) eight-vegetable juice*
>
> *1 small jalapeño chile, seeded and chopped*
>
> *2 tablespoons cold water*
>
> *2 teaspoons cornstarch*

Heat oven to 375°. Grease rack of broiler pan. Place drumsticks on rack in broiler pan. Brush with 1 tablespoon oil. Bake uncovered 1 to 1¼

Turkey Thigh Fajitas

2 turkey thighs (about 2 pounds)

¼ cup olive or vegetable oil

¼ cup lime juice

1 teaspoon chile powder

½ teaspoon red pepper sauce

12 flour tortillas (8 inches in diameter)

1 tablespoon vegetable oil

2 cups julienne strips zucchini (about 1 medium)

2 cups julienne strips yellow summer squash (about 1 medium)

2 large onions, thinly sliced

Remove skin from thighs. Cut turkey into bite-size pieces, removing bone, fat and cartilage. Mix turkey, olive oil, lime juice, chile powder and pepper sauce in glass bowl or sealable heavy-duty plastic bag. Cover bowl or seal bag tightly. Refrigerate at least 2 hours, stirring or turning occasionally.

Heat oven to 325°. Wrap tortillas in aluminum foil. Heat in oven about 15 minutes or until warm. Meanwhile, remove turkey from marinade; discard marinade. Pat turkey dry with paper towels. Heat vegetable oil in 12-inch skillet over medium-high heat until hot. Cook turkey in oil 3 to 4 minutes, stirring occasionally, until turkey is no longer pink in center. Stir in remaining ingredients. Cook about 6 minutes, stirring occasionally, until vegetables are crisp-tender; drain if necessary.

Spoon turkey mixture onto center of each tortilla. Top with shredded cheese, guacamole, sour cream or salsa, if desired. Fold tortilla over filling. *6 servings.*

NUTRITION INFORMATION PER SERVING

1 serving		*Percent of U.S. RDA*	
Calories	515	Vitamin A	4%
Protein, g	33	Vitamin C	6%
Carbohydrate, g	53	Calcium	8%
Fat, g	21	Iron	28%
Cholesterol, mg	90		
Sodium, mg	410		

Creamy Turkey Thighs with Vegetables

2 turkey thighs (about 2 pounds)

2 medium carrots, cut into 1-inch pieces

2 medium potatoes, cut into fourths

1 medium onion, cut into fourths

1 tablespoon chopped fresh or 1 teaspoon dried marjoram leaves

¼ teaspoon pepper

2 cloves garlic, finely chopped

1 can (10¾ ounces) condensed cream of mushroom soup

1 can (4 ounces) mushroom stems and pieces, drained

Heat oven to 350°. Place thighs, carrots, potatoes and onion in ungreased 3-quart casserole. Mix remaining ingredients; spoon over turkey and vegetables. Cover and bake 1 hour 15 minutes to 1 hour 30 minutes, spooning sauce over turkey occasionally, until juice of turkey is no longer pink when centers of thickest pieces are cut and vegetables are tender. *4 servings.*

NUTRITION INFORMATION PER SERVING

1 serving		*Percent of U.S. RDA*	
Calories	450	Vitamin A	58%
Protein, g	46	Vitamin C	8%
Carbohydrate, g	26	Calcium	6%
Fat, g	20	Iron	16%
Cholesterol, mg	120		
Sodium, mg	860		

CHAPTER
5

Wings

Did you think that turkey and chicken wings were just for appetizers? Well, think again! While wings are always a crowd pleaser at parties and buffets, they can be satisfying main dishes as well. For example, you can serve Chinese Chicken Wings as an appetizer, or as a main dish for four—you can even cook them on the grill. To see wings in a whole new light, try Easy Chicken Cacciatore or Mexican Turkey Wing Fricassee, complete with Cornmeal Dumplings. You can let your imagination take wing with these great recipes!

Buffalo Chicken Wings (page 138)

Buffalo Chicken Wings

Blue Cheese Dressing (right)

12 chicken wings (about 2 pounds)

Vegetable oil

2 tablespoons margarine or butter, melted

1 tablespoon white vinegar

2 to 3 teaspoons red pepper sauce

¼ teaspoon salt

Celery, carrot and zucchini sticks

Prepare Blue Cheese Dressing. Cut each wing at joints to make 3 pieces; discard tip. Cut off excess skin; discard.

Heat oven to 275°. Heat oil (2 to 3 inches) in deep fryer or Dutch oven to 375°. Fry 4 to 6 chicken pieces at a time in oil 8 to 10 minutes, turning occasionally, until golden brown and juice of chicken is no longer pink when centers of thickest pieces are cut; drain. Keep warm in oven on cookie sheet while frying remaining chicken. Mix margarine, vinegar, pepper sauce and salt in large bowl until well blended. Add chicken; toss. Serve with dressing and vegetable sticks. *24 appetizers.*

BLUE CHEESE DRESSING

¾ cup crumbled blue cheese (4 ounces)

1 package (3 ounces) cream cheese, softened

½ cup mayonnaise or salad dressing

⅓ cup half-and-half

Reserve ¼ cup of the blue cheese. Beat remaining blue cheese and the cream cheese in small bowl on low speed until blended. Add mayonnaise and half-and-half; beat on low speed until creamy. Stir in reserved blue cheese. Cover and refrigerate at least 3 hours.

OVEN-FRIED CHICKEN WINGS: Heat oven to 425°. Omit vegetable oil. Heat 2 tablespoons margarine or butter in rectangular pan, 13×9×2 inches, in oven until melted. Coat chicken pieces with ¼ cup all-purpose flour; shake off excess flour. Place in pan. Bake uncovered 20 minutes; turn chicken. Bake uncovered 10 to 12 minutes longer or until light golden brown on outside and juice of chicken is no longer pink when centers of thickest pieces are cut; drain. Decrease 2 tablespoons margarine in pepper sauce mixture to 1 tablespoon.

NUTRITION INFORMATION PER SERVING

1 appetizer		Percent of U.S. RDA	
Calories	125	Vitamin A	8%
Protein, g	5	Vitamin C	*
Carbohydrate, g	1	Calcium	4%
Fat, g	11	Iron	2%
Cholesterol, mg	25		
Sodium, mg	150		

Quick Barbecued Chicken Drummettes

2 pounds chicken drummettes
½ cup chile sauce
1 tablespoon honey
1 tablespoon soy sauce
½ teaspoon ground mustard
¼ teaspoon ground red pepper (cayenne)

Place drummettes in 10-inch nonstick skillet. Mix remaining ingredients; spoon over chicken. Heat to boiling; reduce heat to medium-low. Cover and cook 20 to 25 minutes, stirring occasionally, until juice of chicken is no longer pink when centers of thickest pieces are cut. *About 12 appetizers.*

NUTRITION INFORMATION PER SERVING

1 appetizer		*Percent of U.S. RDA*	
Calories	45	Vitamin A	2%
Protein, g	3	Vitamin C	*
Carbohydrate, g	1	Calcium	*
Fat, g	3	Iron	*
Cholesterol, mg	15		
Sodium, mg	80		

Chinese Chicken Wings

To make quick work of cutting up the chicken wings, use poultry shears.

12 chicken wings (about 2½ pounds)
¼ cup plum sauce or plum preserves
2 tablespoons hoisin sauce
½ teaspoon ground ginger
1 clove garlic, finely chopped

Heat oven to 425°. Grease jelly roll pan, 15½×10½×1 inch or large cookie sheet. Cut each wing at joints to make 3 pieces; discard tip. Cut off excess skin; discard. Place chicken in pan.

Bake uncovered 15 minutes; turn chicken. Bake uncovered 5 minutes longer. Mix remaining ingredients; brush on chicken. Bake uncovered 15 minutes longer, brushing once with plum sauce mixture, until juice of chicken is no longer pink when centers of thickest pieces are cut. *4 main-dish servings or 24 appetizers.*

TO GRILL: Cover and grill chicken about 5 inches from medium coals 10 minutes; turn chicken. Brush with plum sauce mixture. Cover and grill 2 to 8 minutes longer, brushing once with plum sauce mixture, until juice of chicken is no longer pink when centers of thickest pieces are cut.

NUTRITION INFORMATION PER SERVING

1 serving		*Percent of U.S. RDA*	
Calories	355	Vitamin A	12%
Protein, g	27	Vitamin C	*
Carbohydrate, g	15	Calcium	2%
Fat, g	21	Iron	10%
Cholesterol, mg	90		
Sodium, mg	440		

Fruity Chicken Wings

12 chicken wings (about 2½ pounds)

1 cup chicken broth

¼ cup dry white wine or apple juice

¼ cup thinly sliced green onions (2 to 3 medium)

1½ tablespoons chopped fresh or 1½ teaspoons dried thyme leaves

2 cloves garlic, finely chopped

2 teaspoons cornstarch

½ teaspoon sugar

¼ cup diced dried fruit and raisin mixture

2 cups hot cooked rice

Cut each wing at joints to make 3 pieces; discard tip. Cut off excess skin; discard. Mix, broth, wine, green onions, thyme and garlic in sealable heavy-duty plastic bag or large glass bowl. Add chicken; turn to coat with marinade. Seal bag or cover dish; refrigerate at least 2 to 4 hours, turning occasionally.

Heat oven to 375°. Grease rack of broiler pan. Remove chicken from marinade; reserve marinade. Place chicken on rack in broiler pan. Bake uncovered 20 minutes; turn chicken. Bake 10 to 12 minutes longer or until juice of chicken is no longer pink when centers of thickest pieces are cut.

Mix ¼ cup of the reserved marinade, the cornstarch and sugar in 1½-quart saucepan. Stir in remaining marinade and the fruit mixture. Heat to boiling, stirring constantly. Boil and stir about 1 minute or until thickened. Serve fruit sauce and chicken over rice. *4 servings.*

TO GRILL: Cover and grill marinated chicken about 4 to 6 inches from medium coals 12 to 18 minutes, turning once or until juice of chicken is no longer pink when centers of thickest pieces are cut.

NUTRITION INFORMATION PER SERVING

1 serving		Percent of U.S. RDA	
Calories	465	Vitamin A	12%
Protein, g	31	Vitamin C	*
Carbohydrate, g	38	Calcium	6%
Fat, g	22	Iron	20%
Cholesterol, mg	90		
Sodium, mg	680		

Fruity Chicken Wings

Crispy Oven-fried Chicken Wings

Sapsago is a hard, grating cheese with a tangy herb flavor.

12 chicken wings (about 2½ pounds)

¾ cup freshly grated sapsago or Parmesan cheese (2 ounces)

⅔ cup dry bread crumbs

2 tablespoons chopped fresh parsley

2 tablespoons chopped fresh or 1 teaspoon dried basil leaves

1 tablespoon chopped fresh or ½ teaspoon dried rosemary leaves

⅓ cup margarine or butter, melted

Heat oven to 425°. Grease jelly roll pan, 15½×10½×1 inch, or large cookie sheet. Cut each wing at joints to make 3 pieces; discard tip. Cut off excess skin; discard. Mix cheese, bread crumbs, parsley, basil and rosemary. Brush chicken with margarine; coat with bread crumb mixture. Place in pan.

Bake uncovered 15 minutes; turn chicken. Bake uncovered about 15 minutes longer or until juice of chicken is no longer pink when centers of thickest pieces are cut. *4 main-dish servings or 24 appetizers.*

NUTRITION INFORMATION PER SERVING

1 appetizer		Percent of U.S. RDA	
Calories	490	Vitamin A	30%
Protein, g	33	Vitamin C	2%
Carbohydrate, g	7	Calcium	24%
Fat, g	37	Iron	12%
Cholesterol, mg	100		
Sodium, mg	550		

Crispy Oven-fried Chicken Wings

Easy Chicken Cacciatore

You'll love this simple version of traditional cacciatore.

12 chicken wings (about 2½ pounds)

1 can (14½ ounces) stewed tomatoes, undrained

1 cup thinly sliced carrots (about 2 medium)

1 cup spaghetti sauce

1 cup sliced zucchini (about 1 small)

2 cups hot cooked instant brown rice

Cut each wing at joints to make 3 pieces; discard tip. Cut off excess skin; discard. Mix chicken, tomatoes, carrots and spaghetti sauce in Dutch oven. Heat to boiling; reduce heat. Cover and simmer 25 minutes, stirring occasionally. Stir in zucchini. Cover and simmer about 10 minutes, stirring occasionally, until juice of chicken is no longer pink when centers of thickest pieces are cut and zucchini is crisp-tender. Serve over rice. *4 servings.*

NUTRITION INFORMATION PER SERVING

1 serving		Percent of U.S. RDA	
Calories	475	Vitamin A	76%
Protein, g	31	Vitamin C	20%
Carbohydrate, g	37	Calcium	8%
Fat, g	25	Iron	18%
Cholesterol, mg	90		
Sodium, mg	950		

Spicy Peach Drummettes

1 tablespoon orange juice concentrate

2 teaspoons apple pie spice

1 teaspoon grated fresh gingerroot

¼ teaspoon salt

1 jar (12 ounces) peach preserves

2 pounds chicken drummettes

Mix all ingredients except drummettes in sealable heavy-duty plastic bag or large glass bowl. Add chicken; turn to coat with marinade. Seal bag or cover dish; refrigerate 2 to 4 hours, turning occasionally.

Heat oven to 425°. Grease jelly roll pan, 15½×10½×1 inch, or rack of broiler pan. Remove chicken from marinade; reserve marinade. Place chicken in pan or on rack in broiler pan. Bake uncovered 15 minutes. Brush chicken with half of marinade. Turn chicken; brush with remaining marinade. Bake uncovered 15 minutes longer or until juice of chicken is no longer pink when centers of thickest pieces are cut. *About 12 appetizers.*

NUTRITION INFORMATION PER SERVING

1 appetizer		Percent of U.S. RDA	
Calories	160	Vitamin A	*
Protein, g	10	Vitamin C	*
Carbohydrate, g	19	Calcium	2%
Fat, g	5	Iron	4%
Cholesterol, mg	30		
Sodium, mg	85		

Rye-Cornmeal Wings

You can also make these wings with whole wheat or round buttery crackers.

12 chicken wings (about 2½ pounds)

¾ cup finely crushed rye crackers

¼ cup yellow cornmeal

1½ teaspoons poultry seasoning

½ teaspoon onion powder

¼ teaspoon pepper

⅓ cup margarine or butter, melted

Heat oven to 425°. Grease jelly roll pan, 15½×10½×1 inch, or large cookie sheet. Cut each wing at joints to make 3 pieces; discard tip. Cut off excess skin; discard. Mix remaining ingredients except margarine. Dip chicken into margarine; coat with cracker crumb mixture. Place in pan.

Bake uncovered 15 minutes; turn chicken. Bake uncovered about 15 minutes longer or until juice of chicken is no longer pink when centers of thickest pieces are cut. *24 appetizers.*

NUTRITION INFORMATION PER SERVING

1 appetizer		Percent of U.S. RDA	
Calories	80	Vitamin A	4%
Protein, g	4	Vitamin C	*
Carbohydrate, g	3	Calcium	*
Fat, g	6	Iron	2%
Cholesterol, mg	15		
Sodium, mg	60		

Peanutty Drummettes

⅓ cup finely chopped dry-roasted peanuts or pecans

⅓ cup dry bread crumbs

1 teaspoon ground coriander

½ teaspoon garlic powder

3 tablespoons margarine or butter, melted

2 tablespoons Worcestershire sauce

2 pounds chicken drummettes

Heat oven to 425°. Grease jelly roll pan, 15½×10½×1 inch, or large cookie sheet. Mix peanuts, bread crumbs, coriander and garlic powder. Mix margarine and Worcestershire sauce. Dip drummettes into margarine mixture; coat with peanut mixture. Place in pan.

Bake uncovered 15 minutes; turn chicken. Bake uncovered about 15 minutes longer or until juice of chicken is no longer pink when centers of thickest pieces are cut. *About 12 appetizers.*

NUTRITION INFORMATION PER SERVING

1 appetizer		*Percent of U.S. RDA*	
Calories	145	Vitamin A	6%
Protein, g	8	Vitamin C	*
Carbohydrate, g	3	Calcium	2%
Fat, g	11	Iron	4%
Cholesterol, mg	25		
Sodium, mg	120		

Honey-Lime Drummettes

2 pounds chicken drummettes

¼ cup honey

1 teaspoon grated lime peel

2 tablespoons lime juice

1 clove garlic, finely chopped

Place chicken drummettes in ungreased rectangular baking dish, 11×7×1½ inches. Mix remaining ingredients; pour over chicken. Cover and refrigerate at least 2 hours.

Set oven control to broil. Remove chicken from marinade; reserve marinade. Place chicken on rack in broiler pan. Broil with tops 4 to 6 inches from heat 10 to 12 minutes, turning once and brushing frequently with marinade, until juice is no longer pink when centers of thickest pieces are cut. Discard any remaining marinade. *12 appetizers.*

NUTRITION INFORMATION PER SERVING

1 serving		*Percent of U.S. RDA*	
Calories	110	Vitamin A	*
Protein, g	10	Vitamin C	*
Carbohydrate, g	6	Calcium	*
Fat, g	5	Iron	4%
Cholesterol, mg	35		
Sodium, mg	30		

Horseradish-sauced Chicken Drummettes

Horseradish comes in several forms—creamy, prepared and in a sauce. This recipe uses prepared horseradish, which you can find in your grocer's refrigerator case.

2 pounds chicken drummettes

¾ cup chicken broth

½ cup chopped onion (about 1 medium)

1 teaspoon ground coriander

¼ teaspoon salt

¼ teaspoon pepper

1 bay leaf

¾ cup sour cream

2 tablespoons all-purpose flour

1 teaspoon prepared horseradish

Place drummettes, broth, onion, coriander, salt, pepper and bay leaf in 12-inch skillet. Heat to boiling; reduce heat. Cover and simmer 20 to 25 minutes, stirring occasionally, until juice of chicken is no longer pink when centers of thickest pieces are cut. Remove chicken from skillet; discard bay leaf.

Mix sour cream, flour and horseradish; stir into broth mixture in skillet. Cook over medium heat, stirring constantly until thickened; continue cooking 1 minute (do not boil). Stir in chicken until coated with sauce. *About 12 appetizers.*

NUTRITION INFORMATION PER SERVING

1 appetizer		*Percent of U.S. RDA*	
Calories	130	Vitamin A	4%
Protein, g	8	Vitamin C	*
Carbohydrate, g	2	Calcium	2%
Fat, g	9	Iron	2%
Cholesterol, mg	35		
Sodium, mg	125		

Sesame Chicken Drummettes

When you're in a hurry, use bottled barbecue sauce in place of this homemade sauce.

3 tablespoons vegetable oil

2 teaspoons sesame oil

½ cup grated Parmesan cheese

⅓ cup all-purpose flour

¼ cup sesame seed, toasted

1½ teaspoons onion powder

¼ teaspoon pepper

2 pounds chicken drummettes

½ cup ketchup

2 tablespoons molasses

1 tablespoon brown or Dijon mustard

Heat oven to 425°. Grease jelly roll pan, 15½×10½×1 inch, or large cookie sheet. Mix vegetable and sesame oils. Mix cheese, flour, sesame seed, onion powder and pepper. Dip drummettes into oil mixture; coat with cheese mixture. Place in pan.

Bake uncovered 15 minutes; turn chicken. Bake uncovered about 15 minutes longer or until juice of chicken is no longer pink when centers of thickest pieces are cut. Heat ketchup, molasses and mustard in 1-quart saucepan until warm. Serve with chicken. *About 12 appetizers.*

NUTRITION INFORMATION PER SERVING

1 appetizer		*Percent of U.S. RDA*	
Calories	190	Vitamin A	4%
Protein, g	10	Vitamin C	*
Carbohydrate, g	8	Calcium	6%
Fat, g	13	Iron	6%
Cholesterol, mg	30		
Sodium, mg	220		

Mexican Turkey Wing Fricassee

If you'd like to make this recipe with chicken drumsticks, use 8 drumsticks (about 2 pounds) and simmer the chicken only 30 minutes before adding the dumplings.

> *2 pounds turkey wings*
>
> *¼ cup all-purpose flour*
>
> *½ teaspoon ground cumin*
>
> *¼ teaspoon salt*
>
> *¼ teaspoon pepper*
>
> *1 tablespoon vegetable oil*
>
> *1½ cups chicken broth*
>
> *1 can (4 ounces) chopped green chiles, drained*
>
> *Cornmeal Dumplings (right)*
>
> *2 tablespoons margarine or butter*
>
> *2 tablespoons all-purpose flour*
>
> *Milk*

Cut each wing at joints to make 3 pieces; discard tip. Mix ¼ cup flour, the cumin, salt and pepper in shallow bowl. Coat turkey with flour mixture. Heat oil in 10-inch skillet over medium heat until hot. Cook turkey in oil until brown on all sides; drain. Add broth and chiles. Heat to boiling; reduce heat. Cover and simmer about 50 minutes, stirring occasionally, until juice of turkey is no longer pink when centers of thickest pieces are cut.

Prepare Cornmeal Dumplings. Remove turkey from Dutch oven; keep warm. Drain liquid from Dutch oven; reserve. Heat margarine in Dutch oven until melted. Stir in 2 tablespoons flour.

Cook over medium heat, stirring constantly, until mixture is smooth and bubbly; remove from heat. Add enough milk to reserved liquid to measure 2 cups; pour into Dutch oven. Heat to boiling, stirring constantly. Boil and stir 1 minute. Return turkey to Dutch oven.

Drop dumpling dough by 4 spoonfuls onto hot turkey (do not drop directly into liquid). Cook uncovered 10 minutes. Cover and cook 10 minutes longer or until toothpick inserted in center of dumpling comes out clean. Garnish with chopped green onions, if desired. *4 servings.*

CORNMEAL DUMPLINGS

> *½ cup all-purpose flour*
>
> *⅓ cup yellow cornmeal*
>
> *2 teaspoons baking powder*
>
> *¼ teaspoon chile powder*
>
> *1 egg, beaten*
>
> *3 tablespoons chicken broth*
>
> *2 tablespoons vegetable oil*

Mix flour, cornmeal, baking powder and chile powder in small bowl. Mix egg, broth and oil; stir into flour mixture until dry ingredients are moistened.

NUTRITION INFORMATION PER SERVING

1 serving		*Percent of U.S. RDA*	
Calories	615	Vitamin A	20%
Protein, g	40	Vitamin C	16%
Carbohydrate, g	37	Calcium	28%
Fat, g	35	Iron	24%
Cholesterol, mg	160		
Sodium, mg	1200		

Mexican Turkey Wing Fricassee

CHAPTER
6

Convenience Cuts

Convenience cuts make it even easier to cook poultry, and range from chicken precut for stir-fries to ground turkey to chicken livers. All these cuts trim prep time, so that you can get dinner on the table more quickly. You'll love Warm Cashew-Chicken Salad prepared with chicken breast tenders, Pizza Rustica, made with ground turkey and Chicken-Apple Pâté made with chicken livers and skinless boneless chicken breasts.

This chapter also includes a section on stir-fries that shows how you can use convenience cuts—skinless boneless chicken, turkey tenders or turkey slices and precut vegetables to have a tasty meal on the table in minutes. You'll find the combinations to be delicious, inventive, and sure to please!

Southwest Chicken Pizza (page 169)

Rumaki

¼ cup soy sauce

2 tablespoons packed brown sugar

*2 thin slices gingerroot or ⅛ teaspoon
   ground ginger*

1 clove garlic, crushed

*½ pound chicken livers, cut in half (about
   10 whole livers)*

*½ can (8-ounce size) whole water
   chestnuts (about 10 whole), drained
   and cut in half*

10 slices bacon, cut in half

Mix soy sauce, brown sugar, gingerroot and garlic in glass or plastic bowl. Stir in livers and water
chestnuts. Cover and refrigerate at least 2 to 4
hours, stirring occasionally.

Heat oven to 400°. Drain chicken; discard marinade. Wrap a piece of bacon around each piece of
liver and a water chestnut. Secure with toothpick.
Place on rack in broiler pan. Bake uncovered 25
to 30 minutes, turning once, until bacon is crisp.
20 appetizers.

NUTRITION INFORMATION PER SERVING

1 appetizer		Percent of U.S. RDA	
Calories	40	Vitamin A	46%
Protein, g	3	Vitamin C	*
Carbohydrate, g	2	Calcium	*
Fat, g	2	Iron	6%
Cholesterol, mg	65		
Sodium, mg	260		

Chicken-Apple Pâté

1 pound chicken livers

*½ pound skinless boneless chicken
   breasts*

1 small onion, cut in half

¼ cup half-and-half

¼ cup bourbon or chicken broth

1 teaspoon salt

½ teaspoon ground nutmeg

2 eggs

1 cup shredded peeled apple (1 medium)

Heat oven to 350°. Grease loaf pan, 8½×4½×2½
inches or 4-cup ovenproof glass mold or porce-
lain terrine. Place chicken livers, chicken breasts
and onion in food processor. Cover and process
until coarsely ground. Add remaining ingredients
except apple. Cover and process until well
blended. Stir in apple.

Pour chicken mixture into mold. Cover tightly
and bake 60 to 70 minutes or until meat thermometer inserted in center reads 180°. Let stand uncovered 1 hour at room temperature. Cover and
refrigerate 2 hours to set. Unmold onto serving
platter.

Garnish with red onion or apple slices if desired.
Serve with bread slices or crackers. *8 servings.*

NUTRITION INFORMATION PER SERVING

1 serving		Percent of U.S. RDA	
Calories	125	Vitamin A	100%
Protein, g	16	Vitamin C	*
Carbohydrate, g	4	Calcium	2%
Fat, g	5	Iron	18%
Cholesterol, mg	290		
Sodium, mg	320		

Chicken-Apple Pâté

Chinese Firecrackers

1 teaspoon vegetable oil

½ pound ground turkey

1 cup finely chopped cabbage

½ cup shredded carrot (about 1 small)

2 tablespoons finely chopped green onion

1 tablespoon chile puree

1 tablespoon dry white wine or chicken broth

1 teaspoon cornstarch

6 frozen phyllo sheets (18×14 inches), thawed

1 tablespoon plus 1 teaspoon vegetable oil

¾ cup sweet-and-sour sauce

Heat 1 teaspoon oil in 10-inch nonstick skillet over medium heat until hot. Cook ground turkey, cabbage, carrot and green onion in oil about 5 minutes, stirring occasionally, until turkey is no longer pink and vegetables are crisp-tender. Stir in chile puree. Mix wine and cornstarch; stir into turkey mixture. Cook uncovered, stirring occasionally, until slightly thickened.

Heat oven to 375°. Cut phyllo sheets crosswise in half, forming two 14×9-inch rectangles. Cut each rectangle lengthwise in half, forming four 14×4½-inch strips. Cover phyllo with damp towel to keep from drying out. Place 1 piece of phyllo on flat surface. Brush with small amount of oil. Top with another piece of phyllo. Place about 1 tablespoon turkey mixture on 1 short end of phyllo; roll up from short end. Twist phyllo 1 inch from each end to form firecracker shape. Repeat with remaining phyllo and turkey mixture. Brush firecrackers with remaining oil. Place on ungreased cookie sheet.

Bake 18 to 22 minutes or until phyllo is crisp and golden brown. Serve with sweet-and-sour sauce. *12 appetizers.*

NUTRITION INFORMATION PER SERVING

1 appetizer		*Percent of U.S. RDA*	
Calories	105	Vitamin A	10%
Protein, g	5	Vitamin C	2%
Carbohydrate, g	13	Calcium	*
Fat, g	4	Iron	4%
Cholesterol, mg	15		
Sodium, mg	100		

Oriental Chicken Salad

Tahini paste is made from ground sesame seed and is found in many Oriental grocery stores or other specialty stores.

*1 package (3 ounces) Oriental flavor
    ramen-noodle soup mix*

Tahini Dressing (right)

*3 cups uncooked rotelle (corkscrew
    shape) pasta*

2 teaspoons sesame or vegetable oil

*1 pound skinless boneless chicken breasts,
    cut into 1-inch strips*

2 green onions, chopped

*1 package (10 ounces) frozen sugar snap
    peas, thawed*

*1 can (11 ounces) mandarin orange
    segments, drained*

Remove seasoning packet from soup mix to use in dressing; reserve ramen noodles. Prepare Tahini Dressing. Cook rotelle as directed on package; drain. Meanwhile, heat oil in 10-inch skillet over medium-high heat until hot. Cook chicken in oil 6 to 8 minutes, stirring occasionally, until chicken is no longer pink in center; remove from heat. Drain rotelle. Break block of ramen noodles. Mix rotelle, chicken, ramen noodles and remaining ingredients in large bowl. Pour dressing over salad; toss. Serve warm. *6 servings.*

TAHINI DRESSING

⅓ cup tahini paste or peanut butter

¼ cup vegetable oil

2 tablespoons lemon juice

4 to 6 drops red pepper sauce

*Reserved seasoning packet from ramen
    noodles*

Mix all ingredients.

NUTRITION INFORMATION PER SERVING

1 serving		Percent of U.S. RDA	
Calories	595	Vitamin A	*
Protein, g	30	Vitamin C	26%
Carbohydrate, g	72	Calcium	10%
Fat, g	23	Iron	32%
Cholesterol, mg	40		
Sodium, mg	640		

Warm Cashew-Chicken Salad

This easy salad topped with crunchy cashews can also be served cold. You can use napa cabbage, bok choy or Romaine lettuce as a crunchy base for the chicken.

2 teaspoons vegetable oil

1 pound chicken breast tenders, cut into 1-inch pieces

1 cup finely chopped celery (about 2 medium stalks)

¼ cup finely chopped onion (about 1 small)

¼ cup light olive oil

2 tablespoons tarragon vinegar

1 tablespoon chopped fresh or 1 teaspoon dried tarragon leaves

3 cups shredded napa (Chinese) cabbage

½ cup cashews

Heat 2 teaspoons oil in 10-inch skillet over medium-high heat until hot. Cook chicken, celery and onion in oil about 8 minutes, stirring occasionally, until chicken is no longer pink in center. Mix ¼ cup oil, the vinegar and tarragon; pour over chicken mixture. Serve over cabbage. Top with cashews. *6 servings.*

NUTRITION INFORMATION PER SERVING

1 serving		Percent of U.S. RDA	
Calories	255	Vitamin A	10%
Protein, g	19	Vitamin C	14%
Carbohydrate, g	5	Calcium	6%
Fat, g	18	Iron	8%
Cholesterol, mg	40		
Sodium, mg	140		

Warm Oriental Turkey Salad

3 tablespoons soy sauce

3 tablespoons honey

1 tablespoon lemon juice

1 tablespoon vegetable oil

1 teaspoon finely chopped gingerroot or ¼ teaspoon ground ginger

2 green onions, sliced

2 cloves garlic, finely chopped

4 turkey breast slices (about 1 pound)

4 cups shredded Napa (Chinese) cabbage

1 cup shredded carrots (about 1½ medium)

½ cup chow mein noodles

Mix all ingredients except turkey, cabbage, carrots and noodles in glass or plastic bowl or plastic bag. Add turkey slices; turn to coat with marinade. Cover dish or seal bag tightly. Refrigerate at least 4 hours. Remove turkey slices; reserve marinade. Heat marinade to boiling in 1-quart saucepan; boil 1 minute.

Set oven control to broil. Place turkey on rack in broiler pan. Broil with tops 4 to 6 inches from heat 6 to 8 minutes, turning once, until no longer pink in center. Cut turkey into ¼-inch strips. Mix turkey, cabbage, carrots and noodles in large bowl. Add marinade; toss to coat. *4 servings.*

NUTRITION INFORMATION PER SERVING

1 serving		Percent of U.S. RDA	
Calories	290	Vitamin A	64%
Protein, g	29	Vitamin C	30%
Carbohydrate, g	23	Calcium	10%
Fat, g	9	Iron	14%
Cholesterol, mg	70		
Sodium, mg	920		

Turkey Salad Niçoise

Dijon Vinaigrette (right)

4 medium new potatoes, cut into fourths

1 package (10 ounces) frozen whole green beans, thawed

2 teaspoons vegetable oil

1 pound turkey breast slices, cut into 1-inch strips

¼ teaspoon salt

6 cups bite-size pieces Bibb lettuce

2 medium tomatoes, cut into wedges

2 hard-cooked eggs, cut into wedges

¼ cup pitted ripe olives

Prepare Dijon Vinaigrette. Place potatoes and enough water to cover in 2-quart saucepan. Heat to boiling. Cook over medium heat 10 to 15 minutes or until potatoes are almost tender. Add green beans. Cook 5 minutes longer; drain.

Heat oil in 10-inch skillet over medium-high heat until hot. Cook turkey and salt in oil 8 to 10 minutes, stirring occasionally, until turkey is no longer pink in center; remove from heat.

Arrange lettuce on large serving platter. Top with turkey. Arrange potatoes, green beans, tomatoes, eggs and olives around edge of platter. Drizzle with Dijon Vinaigrette. Serve warm. *6 servings.*

DIJON VINAIGRETTE

⅔ cup vegetable oil

¼ cup tarragon vinegar

2 teaspoons Dijon mustard

1 tablespoon chopped fresh or 1 teaspoon dried tarragon leaves

Mix all ingredients.

NUTRITION INFORMATION PER SERVING

1 serving		*Percent of U.S. RDA*	
Calories	425	Vitamin A	10%
Protein, g	22	Vitamin C	16%
Carbohydrate, g	21	Calcium	6%
Fat, g	30	Iron	16%
Cholesterol, mg	115		
Sodium, mg	240		

Sizzling Stir-fries

With pre-cut vegetables, and chicken in the refrigerator, you can get a jump on preparing quick and creative stir-fry combinations that rival take-out food!

DIRECTIONS:

Heat wok or 12-inch skillet over high heat until hot. Add 1 tablespoon vegetable oil; rotate wok to coat side. Add chicken or turkey. Stir-fry until no longer pink in center; remove from wok. Add 1 tablespoon vegetable oil to wok; rotate wok to coat side. Add vegetables or fruit and any Additional Ingredients as indicated from chart below. Stir-fry about 2 to 6 minutes or until crisp-tender. Add chicken and sauce and any Additional Ingredients as indicated from chart below. Cook and stir about 2 minutes or until heated through. Serve with Accompaniments suggested in chart below.

SUPER-EASY STIR-FRY CHART

Chicken or Turkey
(choose 1)

1 pound skinless boneless chicken breast halves or thighs, cut into 1-inch pieces	*or* *1 pound turkey tenderloin, cut into 1-inch pieces*	*or* *1 pound turkey slices, cut crosswise into ½-inch strips*

Vegetables and Fruit Additions
(choose any combination to equal 4 cups)

- Asparagus (1-inch pieces)
- Baby corn
- Bamboo shoots
- Bean sprouts
- Bell peppers (¼-inch strips or 1-inch pieces)
- Bok choy (coarsely chopped)
- Broccoli flowerets
- Cabbage (coarsely chopped or shredded)
- Carrots (thin julienne strips or slices)
- Cauliflowerets
- Celery (sliced)
- Chinese (napa) cabbage (coarsely chopped or shredded)
- Frozen vegetables, plain or combinations, thawed

- Green beans (1-inch pieces)
- Jicama (thin julienne strips or slices)
- Mushrooms (halved or sliced)
- Mandarin orange segments
- Onions (coarsely chopped or 1-inch pieces of green onion)
- Pea pods (remove strings)
- Pineapple chunks
- Sugar snap peas
- Tomato wedges (seeded)
- Water chestnuts (sliced)
- Yellow summer squash (thin julienne strips or slices)
- Zucchini (thin julienne strips or slices)

Sauce
(choose 1 using ½ cup)

- Duck sauce
- Hoisin sauce
- Oyster sauce
- Plum sauce
- Stir-fry sauce
- Sweet-and-sour sauce
- Teryaki marinade and sauce
- Purchased marinade sauce, any flavor

Additional Ingredients

- Garlic (1 to 2 cloves, finely chopped). Add with vegetables.
- Gingerroot (finely chopped). Add with vegetables.
- Lemon juice, orange juice, pineapple juice or sherry (1 to 2 tablespoons). Add with sauce.
- Nuts (add after sauce addition or as a garnish)

Accompaniments

- Chow mein noodles
- Couscous
- Pasta (Chinese egg noodles, linguini, orzo or vermicelli)
- Rice (regular or instant white or brown)
- Soy sauce

Turkey Club Salad with Hot Bacon Dressing

This salad has all the traditional ingredients found in a club sandwich—turkey, bacon, tomatoes, lettuce, Swiss cheese and croutons for the bread.

6 cups bite-size pieces leaf lettuce

½ pint cherry tomatoes, cut in half

2 teaspoons vegetable oil

1 pound turkey breast slices, cut into 1-inch strips

8 slices bacon

½ cup chopped onion (about 1 medium)

2 teaspoons sugar

½ teaspoon ground mustard

½ teaspoon pepper

½ cup cider vinegar

½ cup flavored croutons

¼ cup shredded Swiss cheese (1 ounce)

Mix lettuce and tomatoes in large bowl. Heat oil in 10-inch skillet over medium-high heat until hot. Cook turkey in oil 6 to 8 minutes, stirring occasionally, until turkey is no longer pink in center. Arrange turkey on lettuce mixture. Cook bacon in same skillet over low heat 8 to 10 minutes, turning occasionally, until crisp and brown. Drain bacon, reserving 2 tablespoons fat in skillet. Crumble bacon; sprinkle over salad.

Cook onion in bacon fat about 2 minutes, stirring occasionally, until crisp-tender. Stir in sugar, mustard, pepper and vinegar. Cook about 2 minutes, stirring occasionally, until hot. Pour onion mixture over salad; toss. Top with croutons and cheese. Serve warm. *4 servings.*

NUTRITION INFORMATION PER SERVING

1 serving		Percent of U.S. RDA	
Calories	355	Vitamin A	6%
Protein, g	42	Vitamin C	14%
Carbohydrate, g	13	Calcium	12%
Fat, g	16	Iron	14%
Cholesterol, mg	105		
Sodium, mg	370		

Turkey Club Salad with Hot Bacon Dressing

Thai Chicken Salad

Sweet-and-Sour Dressing (right)

2 teaspoons vegetable oil

1 pound chicken breast tenders

2 cups julienne strips zucchini (about 1 medium)

1 cup shredded carrots (about 2 medium)

½ cup 1-inch julienne strips green onions

¼ teaspoon crushed red pepper

2 cups chopped bok choy, stems and leaves

¼ cup dry-roasted peanuts

2 tablespoons chopped fresh cilantro

Prepare Sweet-and-Sour Dressing. Heat oil in 10-inch skillet over medium-high heat until hot. Cook chicken in oil 10 to 12 minutes, stirring occasionally, until chicken is no longer pink in center. Stir in zucchini, carrots, green onions and red pepper. Cook about 4 minutes, stirring occasionally, until vegetables are crisp-tender. Stir in dressing; cook 1 minute. Spoon chicken mixture over bok choy. Top with peanuts and cilantro. *4 servings.*

SWEET-AND-SOUR DRESSING

¼ cup vegetable oil

2 tablespoons sugar

2 tablespoons vinegar

¼ teaspoon salt

⅛ teaspoon crushed red pepper

Beat all ingredients, using wire whisk.

NUTRITION INFORMATION PER SERVING

1 serving		Percent of U.S. RDA	
Calories	425	Vitamin A	56%
Protein, g	38	Vitamin C	22%
Carbohydrate, g	15	Calcium	8%
Fat, g	25	Iron	14%
Cholesterol, mg	85		
Sodium, mg	290		

Turkey-Avocado Sandwiches

2 teaspoons vegetable oil

1 pound turkey breast slices

¼ cup ranch dressing

4 slices sourdough bread, ½ inch thick

1 medium avocado, peeled and sliced

4 slices (1 ounce each) mozzarella cheese

Heat oil in 10-inch skillet over medium-high heat until hot. Cook turkey breast slices in oil 10 to 12 minutes, turning once, until turkey is no longer pink in center. Set oven control to broil. Spread dressing over bread. Top with turkey, avocado and cheese. Place on rack in broiler pan. Broil with tops about 3 inches from heat 2 to 4 minutes or until cheese is melted. *4 open-face sandwiches.*

NUTRITION INFORMATION PER SERVING

1 sandwich		Percent of U.S. RDA	
Calories	465	Vitamin A	8%
Protein, g	46	Vitamin C	2%
Carbohydrate, g	19	Calcium	26%
Fat, g	24	Iron	14%
Cholesterol, mg	110		
Sodium, mg	510		

Italian Burgers

1 pound ground turkey

⅓ cup spaghetti sauce

3 tablespoons finely chopped onion

4 slices (1 ounce each) provolone cheese

8 slices Italian bread

Set oven control to broil. Mix ground turkey, spaghetti sauce and onion. Shape mixture into 4 patties, each about ¾ inch thick. Place on rack in broiler pan. Broil with tops about 3 inches from heat 5 to 7 minutes on each side, turning once, until turkey is no longer pink in center. About 1 minute before burgers are done, top each with cheese slice. Broil until cheese is melted. Serve between bread slices. *4 servings.*

TO GRILL: Grease hinged wire grill basket. Place patties in basket. Cover and grill 4 to 6 inches from medium coals 15 to 20 minutes, turning once, until turkey is no longer pink in center. About 1 minute before burgers are done, open grill basket (do not close basket) and top each with cheese slice. Grill until cheese is melted. Serve between bread slices.

NUTRITION INFORMATION PER SERVING

1 serving		Percent of U.S. RDA	
Calories	415	Vitamin A	10%
Protein, g	34	Vitamin C	*
Carbohydrate, g	25	Calcium	26%
Fat, g	21	Iron	16%
Cholesterol, mg	100		
Sodium, mg	710		

Grilled Texas Burgers

1 pound ground turkey

½ cup barbecue sauce

1 can (4 ounces) chopped green chiles, drained

4 slices (1 ounce each) Monterey Jack cheese with jalapeño peppers

4 hamburger buns, split

Set oven control to broil. Mix ground turkey, barbecue sauce and chiles. Shape mixture into 4 patties, each about ¾ inch thick. Place on rack in broiler pan. Broil with tops about 3 inches from heat 10 to 14 minutes, turning once, until turkey is no longer pink in center. About 1 minute before burgers are done, top each with cheese slice. Broil until cheese is melted. Serve on buns. *4 servings.*

TO GRILL: Grill patties covered about 4 to 6 inches from medium coals 14 to 16 minutes, turning once, until turkey is no longer pink in center. About 1 minute before burgers are done, top each with cheese slice. Grill until cheese is melted.

NUTRITION INFORMATION PER SERVING

1 serving		*Percent of U.S. RDA*	
Calories	445	Vitamin A	16%
Protein, g	33	Vitamin C	18%
Carbohydrate, g	29	Calcium	28%
Fat, g	23	Iron	16%
Cholesterol, mg	105		
Sodium, mg	1050		

Grilled Texas Burgers

Sweet-and-Sour Turkey Patties

1½ pounds ground turkey

1 cup soft bread crumbs (about 1½ slices bread)

⅓ cup chicken broth

1 can (8 ounces) crushed pineapple in juice, drained and juice reserved

3 tablespoons sugar

¼ cup white vinegar

1 teaspoon soy sauce

1 small clove garlic, finely chopped

2 tablespoons cornstarch

2 tablespoons cold water

½ cup chopped bell pepper (about 1 small)

Set oven control to broil. Mix ground turkey, breads crumbs and broth. Shape mixture into 6 patties, each about ½ inch thick. Place on rack in broiler pan. Broil with tops about 3 inches from heat about 12 minutes, turning once, until turkey is no longer pink in center.

Add enough water to reserved pineapple juice to measure 1 cup. Heat pineapple juice mixture, sugar, vinegar, soy sauce and garlic to boiling in 2-quart saucepan. Mix cornstarch and water; stir into juice mixture. Boil and stir 1 minute. Stir in pineapple and bell pepper. Serve sauce over patties. *6 servings.*

NUTRITION INFORMATION PER SERVING

1 serving		*Percent of U.S. RDA*	
Calories	275	Vitamin A	2%
Protein, g	24	Vitamin C	8%
Carbohydrate, g	19	Calcium	2%
Fat, g	12	Iron	10%
Cholesterol, mg	75		
Sodium, mg	200		

Mix-and-Match Garden Salad Chart

With a little preplanning and preparation, your refrigerator can hold all of the "fixings" for a bountiful at-home salad bar. Store ingredients separately in covered containers or sealable plastic bags.

DIRECTIONS:

Prepare chicken or turkey as indicated in the chart below. Start by placing salad greens on individual serving plates or in large serving bowl. Top with selections from each category listed in the chart. Each combination will make four servings.

MIX-AND-MATCH GARDEN CHICKEN SALAD CHART

Chicken or Turkey
(choose 1)

- 4 grilled, broiled, sautéed or poached skinless boneless chicken breast halves or turkey breast slices, cut into thin crosswise strips

- 2 grilled, broiled, sautéed or poached turkey breast tenderloins, cut into thin crosswise strips

- 2 cups cubed, chopped or shredded cooked chicken or turkey

Salad Greens
(choose 1½ cups per serving)

- Assorted field greens (chicory, dandelion, mesclun, red oak-leaf, salad burnet, sorrel)

- Assorted young, tender greens (beet, kale, mustard, swiss chard)

- Arugula

- Belgian endive

- Bibb lettuce

- Boston (butterhead) lettuce

- Cabbage (green, red, Chinese or napa)

- Curly endive

- Escarole

- Fresh whole herb leaves (basil, oregano, marjoram, lovage, dill)

- Green or red leaf lettuce

- Iceberg lettuce

- Radicchio

- Romaine

- Spinach

- Watercress

MIX-AND-MATCH GARDEN CHICKEN SALAD CHART (*continued*)

Vegetable and Fruit Additions
(choose ½ to 1 cup per serving)

- Apple
- Artichoke hearts
- Avocado
- Banana
- Bell peppers
- Berries
- Broccoli flowerets
- Cabbage
- Canned fruit
- Carrots
- Cauliflowerets
- Celery

- Cherries
- Corn
- Cucumbers
- Grapefruit
- Grapes
- Kiwifruit
- Mango
- Melon
- Mushrooms
- Nectarine
- Olives
- Onions

- Oranges
- Papaya
- Peaches
- Pears
- Peas
- Pineapple
- Sprouts
- Star fruit (carambola)
- Tomato
- Water chestnuts
- Yellow summer squash
- Zucchini

Dressings

- Homemade or purchased salad dressing (2 to 4 tablespoons per serving)

Toppings

- Bacon
- Chow mein noodles
- Croutons
- Fresh herbs

- Hard-cooked eggs
- Miniature crackers
- Nuts, toasted or plain
- Oyster crackers

- Raisins
- Shredded or diced cheese
- Toasted or fried corn or flour tortilla or wonton strips

Zesty Chicken Patties

Similar to crab cakes, these chicken patties are also nice cooked on the grill. Use a wire grill basket made for burgers.

1¼ cups soft bread crumbs (about 1¾ slices bread)

¼ cup chopped fresh parsley

¼ cup mayonnaise or salad dressing

1 tablespoon Dijon mustard

2 teaspoons chopped fresh or ½ teaspoon dried thyme leaves

¼ cup chopped green onions (2 to 3 medium)

1 egg, beaten

1 pound ground chicken

1 tablespoon margarine or butter

¼ cup horseradish sauce

Mix 1 cup of the bread crumbs, the parsley, mayonnaise, mustard, thyme, green onions, egg and chicken. Shape mixture into 4 patties, each about ¾ inch thick. Coat patties with remaining bread crumbs.

Heat margarine in 10-inch skillet over medium-high heat until melted. Cook patties in margarine 12 to 16 minutes, turning once, until chicken is no longer pink in center and patties are golden brown. Serve with horseradish sauce. *4 servings.*

TO GRILL: Grease hinged wire grill basket. Place patties in basket. Cover and grill 4 to 6 inches from medium coals 15 to 20 minutes, turning once, until chicken is no longer pink in center and patties are golden brown.

NUTRITION INFORMATION PER SERVING

1 serving		Percent of U.S. RDA	
Calories	330	Vitamin A	8%
Protein, g	27	Vitamin C	4%
Carbohydrate, g	9	Calcium	6%
Fat, g	21	Iron	14%
Cholesterol, mg	125		
Sodium, mg	310		

Southwest Chicken Pizza

Prepared Italian bread shells are widely available. If you use a bread shell, your pizza will have a thick, chewy crust.

1 tablespoon vegetable oil

1 pound chicken breast tenders, cut into 1-inch pieces

½ cup chopped onion (about 1 medium)

½ cup chopped red bell pepper (about 1 small)

1 teaspoon chile powder

¼ teaspoon salt

¾ cup chopped tomato (about 1 medium)

1 Italian bread shell or prepared pizza crust (12 inches in diameter)

½ cup salsa

½ cup guacamole

½ cup sour cream

Heat oven to 400°. Heat oil in 10-inch skillet over medium-high heat until hot. Cook chicken, onion, bell pepper, chile powder and salt in oil about 8 minutes, stirring occasionally, until chicken is no longer pink in center. Sprinkle tomato over bread shell. Top with chicken mixture. Place on ungreased cookie sheet or 12-inch pizza pan. Bake 12 to 15 minutes or until hot. Top with salsa, guacamole and sour cream. *6 servings.*

NUTRITION INFORMATION PER SERVING

1 slice		Percent of U.S. RDA	
Calories	460	Vitamin A	16%
Protein, g	24	Vitamin C	24%
Carbohydrate, g	52	Calcium	4%
Fat, g	19	Iron	22%
Cholesterol, mg	55		
Sodium, mg	1150		

Pizza Rustica

1 tablespoon olive or vegetable oil

1 pound ground turkey

1 cup peeled and chopped eggplant (about ¼ pound)

1 cup chopped red bell pepper (about 1 medium)

1 cup chopped zucchini (about 1 medium)

1 can (15 ounces) tomato sauce

1 Italian bread shell or prepared pizza crust (12 inches in diameter)

¼ cup grated Parmesan cheese

¼ cup chopped fresh basil leaves

Heat oven to 400°. Heat oil in 10-inch skillet over medium-high heat until hot. Cook turkey, eggplant, bell pepper and zucchini in oil about 8 minutes, stirring occasionally, until turkey is no longer pink; drain. Spread tomato sauce evenly over bread shell. Top with turkey mixture. Sprinkle with Parmesan cheese and basil. Place on ungreased cookie sheet or 12-inch pizza pan. Bake 12 to 15 minutes or until hot. *6 servings.*

NUTRITION INFORMATION PER SERVING

1 slice		Percent of U.S. RDA	
Calories	485	Vitamin A	20%
Protein, g	25	Vitamin C	38%
Carbohydrate, g	57	Calcium	10%
Fat, g	20	Iron	30%
Cholesterol, mg	55		
Sodium, mg	1250		

Turkey with Wine

1 tablespoon margarine or butter

1 clove garlic, finely chopped

Salt to taste

1 pound boneless turkey breast slices, cutlets or tenderloins, ¼ to ½ inch thick

½ cup dry red wine

1 tablespoon tomato paste

3 cups sliced mushrooms (about 8 ounces)

2 tablespoons chopped green onions

Heat margarine and garlic in 12-inch nonstick skillet over medium-high heat until hot. Lightly sprinkle turkey with salt. Cook turkey in margarine 6 to 8 minutes, turning once, until no longer pink in center. Remove turkey from skillet; keep warm.

Mix wine and tomato paste in skillet. Stir in mushrooms. Cook 3 to 5 minutes, stirring occasionally, until mushrooms are tender. Serve mushroom mixture over turkey. Sprinkle with onions. *4 servings.*

Note: If turkey breast tenderloin pieces are too thick, flatten each to ¼-inch thickness between plastic wrap or waxed paper.

NUTRITION INFORMATION PER SERVING

1 serving		Percent of U.S. RDA	
Calories	210	Vitamin A	4%
Protein, g	29	Vitamin C	4%
Carbohydrate, g	8	Calcium	2%
Fat, g	7	Iron	18%
Cholesterol, mg	70		
Sodium, mg	270		

Easy Turkey Cacciatore

Turkey tenderloin slices are just the right size for this no-fuss cacciatore.

1 pound turkey breast slices

¼ cup all-purpose flour

¼ teaspoon pepper

2 tablespoons olive or vegetable oil

1 small onion, sliced

1 small green bell pepper, cut into ¼-inch strips

1 jar (26 ounces) spaghetti sauce

1 package (8 ounces) refrigerated fettuccine

½ cup shredded mozzarella cheese (2 ounces)

Coat turkey breast slices with flour; sprinkle with pepper. Heat oil in 12-inch skillet over medium-high heat until hot. Cook turkey, onion and bell pepper in oil 10 to 12 minutes, turning once, until turkey is no longer pink in center. Stir in spaghetti sauce. Cook about 5 minutes or until sauce is hot.

Cook fettuccine as directed on package; drain. Arrange fettuccine on 4 serving plates. Top with turkey mixture. Sprinkle with cheese. *4 servings.*

NUTRITION INFORMATION PER SERVING

1 serving		Percent of U.S. RDA	
Calories	580	Vitamin A	14%
Protein, g	41	Vitamin C	16%
Carbohydrate, g	63	Calcium	20%
Fat, g	22	Iron	30%
Cholesterol, mg	125		
Sodium, mg	1630		

Three-Cheese Macaroni and Chicken

1 package (7 ounces) elbow macaroni

2 tablespoons margarine or butter

1 pound skinless boneless chicken breast, cut up for stir-fry

2 tablespoons all-purpose flour

½ teaspoon salt

½ teaspoon pepper

2 cups milk

½ cup shredded Cheddar cheese (2 ounces)

½ cup shredded Monterey Jack cheese (2 ounces)

½ cup shredded Swiss cheese (2 ounces)

Cook macaroni as directed on package; drain. Heat margarine in 3-quart saucepan over medium heat until melted. Cook chicken in margarine about 8 minutes, stirring occasionally, until chicken is no longer pink in center. Stir in flour, salt and pepper. Cook, stirring constantly, until mixture is bubbly; remove from heat. Stir in milk. Heat to boiling, stirring constantly. Boil and stir 1 minute; remove from heat. Stir in cheeses until melted. Stir in macaroni. Cook, stirring constantly, until macaroni is coated and mixture is hot. *6 servings.*

NUTRITION INFORMATION PER SERVING

1 serving		*Percent of U.S. RDA*	
Calories	400	Vitamin A	16%
Protein, g	31	Vitamin C	*
Carbohydrate, g	32	Calcium	32%
Fat, g	17	Iron	12%
Cholesterol, mg	75		
Sodium, mg	570		

Curried Turkey Meatballs with Chutney Sauce

Chutney Sauce (below)

1 pound ground turkey or chicken

½ cup crushed cracker crumbs

⅓ cup evaporated skimmed milk

2 tablespoons finely chopped green onions

1½ to 2 teaspoons curry powder

¼ teaspoon salt

Prepare Chutney Sauce. Heat oven to 400°. Mix remaining ingredients. Shape into 48 one-inch balls. Place in lightly greased rectangular pan, 13×9×2 inches. Bake uncovered 10 to 15 minutes or until no longer pink in center. Serve hot with Chutney Sauce. *4 dozen appetizers or 8 main dish servings.*

CHUTNEY SAUCE

½ cup plain nonfat yogurt

1 tablespoon finely chopped chutney

¼ teaspoon curry powder

Mix all ingredients. Cover and refrigerate at least 1 hour to blend flavors.

NUTRITION INFORMATION PER SERVING

1 serving		*Percent of U.S. RDA*	
Calories	20	Vitamin A	*
Protein, g	2	Vitamin C	*
Carbohydrate, g	1	Calcium	*
Fat, g	1	Iron	*
Cholesterol, mg	10		
Sodium, mg	30		

Turkey with Couscous

Couscous is partially cooked semolina wheat that has a mild flavor and a texture similar to rice. It is a staple in many Middle Eastern diets, and here adds interest to turkey breasts.

1 cup orange juice

1 cup water

¼ teaspoon salt

1 cup uncooked couscous

½ cup golden raisins

¼ cup chopped fresh parsley

1 tablespoon grated lemon peel

1 tablespoon lemon juice

2 tablespoons margarine or butter

1 pound turkey breast slices, cut in half

¼ cup orange juice

½ teaspoon ground cinnamon

Heat 1 cup orange juice, the water and salt to boiling in 2-quart saucepan. Stir in couscous. Continue boiling 2 minutes, stirring frequently; remove from heat. Cover and let stand 5 to 10 minutes or until liquid is absorbed. Stir in raisins, parsley, lemon peel and lemon juice.

Heat margarine in 10-inch skillet until melted. Add turkey, ¼ cup orange juice and cinnamon. Cook 10 to 12 minutes, stirring occasionally, until turkey is no longer pink in center. Serve turkey mixture over couscous mixture. *4 servings.*

NUTRITION INFORMATION PER SERVING

1 serving		*Percent of U.S. RDA*	
Calories	450	Vitamin A	10%
Protein, g	33	Vitamin C	32%
Carbohydrate, g	60	Calcium	4%
Fat, g	10	Iron	14%
Cholesterol, mg	65		
Sodium, mg	280		

Turkey Slices with Walnuts

2 tablespoons margarine or butter

4 turkey breast slices (about 1 pound)

¼ teaspoon salt

1 tablespoon margarine or butter

⅓ cup chopped walnuts

2 green onions, sliced

1 teaspoon cornstarch

½ cup dry white wine or chicken broth

1 teaspoon sugar

Melt 2 tablespoons margarine in 12-inch skillet over medium-high heat. Cook turkey slices in margarine 6 to 8 minutes, turning once and sprinkling with salt after turning, until no longer pink in center. Remove turkey from skillet; keep warm.

Add 1 tablespoon margarine to skillet. Cook walnuts and onions in margarine over medium-high heat 2 to 3 minutes, stirring frequently, until onions are tender.

Stir cornstarch into wine; pour into skillet. Stir in sugar. Heat to boiling, stirring constantly. Boil and stir 1 minute. Pour sauce over turkey. *4 servings.*

NUTRITION INFORMATION PER SERVING

1 serving		*Percent of U.S. RDA*	
Calories	290	Vitamin A	12%
Protein, g	28	Vitamin C	*
Carbohydrate, g	4	Calcium	2%
Fat, g	18	Iron	8%
Cholesterol, mg	70		
Sodium, mg	300		

Chicken-Vegetable Lasagne

If ricotta cheese is not available, you can use cottage cheese; whirl it in a blender to create a smooth texture.

1 teaspoon vegetable oil

1 pound ground chicken or turkey

½ cup chopped onion (about 1 medium)

1 clove garlic, finely chopped

1 jar (28 ounces) spaghetti sauce

1 package (16 ounces) lasagne noodles

1 container (15 ounces) ricotta cheese

¼ cup grated Parmesan cheese

2 cups thinly sliced zucchini (about 1 medium)

1 package (10 ounces) frozen chopped spinach, thawed and drained

2 cups shredded mozzarella cheese (8 ounces)

Heat oil in 10-inch skillet over medium-high heat until hot. Cook chicken, onion and garlic in oil 6 to 8 minutes, stirring occasionally, until chicken is no longer pink; drain. Stir in spaghetti sauce; heat through.

Heat oven to 350°. Cook noodles as directed on package; drain. Mix ricotta and Parmesan cheeses. Mix zucchini and spinach. Spread 1 cup of the sauce mixture in ungreased rectangular pan, 13×9×2 inches. Top with 4 noodles. Spread 1 cup of the ricotta cheese mixture over noodles. Top with zucchini mixture. Sprinkle with 1 cup of the mozzarella cheese.

Top with remaining noodles. Spread remaining ricotta cheese mixture over noodles. Spread remaining sauce mixture over cheese mixture. Sprinkle with remaining mozzarella cheese. Cover and bake 30 minutes. Uncover and bake about 15 minutes longer or until hot and bubbly. Let stand 15 minutes before cutting. *8 servings.*

NUTRITION INFORMATION PER SERVING

1 serving		Percent of U.S. RDA	
Calories	565	Vitamin A	36%
Protein, g	36	Vitamin C	8%
Carbohydrate, g	61	Calcium	50%
Fat, g	22	Iron	26%
Cholesterol, mg	75		
Sodium, mg	1220		

CHAPTER
7

Express

Jump on board for a quick ride to a great meal, with our express recipes! Almost all of these recipes use cooked chicken and turkey to make a meal in a flash. Try Chicken Gazpacho Salad, Grilled Stilton and Chicken Sandwiches or Pizza Mexicana to make a quick meal special. These recipes are perfect to use leftover baked or poached chicken and turkey, or if you like, you can buy cooked chicken and turkey at the deli.

We have also included a mix-and-match pasta salad guide, to help you create luscious salads in what seems like seconds. These salads will be welcome all year because they offer a wonderful variety of pasta, grains, vegetables, fruits and dressings to create your favorite combinations. You'll find that while these recipes are fast, they never scrimp on flavor!

Mediterranean Sandwich (page 180)

Chicken Gazpacho Salad

1 package (14 ounces) fusilli pasta

2 cups cubed cooked chicken

1 cup chopped cucumber (about 1 small)

1 cup chopped yellow or red bell pepper (about 1 medium)

1 cup chopped tomato (about 1 large)

¾ cup spicy eight-vegetable juice

¼ cup lemon juice

½ teaspoon freshly ground pepper

¼ teaspoon salt

1 clove garlic, finely chopped

Cook pasta as directed on package; drain. Mix pasta and remaining ingredients. Serve immediately. *6 servings.*

NUTRITION INFORMATION PER SERVING

1 serving		Percent of U.S. RDA	
Calories	360	Vitamin A	14%
Protein, g	23	Vitamin C	30%
Carbohydrate, g	58	Calcium	2%
Fat, g	4	Iron	20%
Cholesterol, mg	40		
Sodium, mg	510		

Fruited Chicken Salad

Try new lemon- or orange-flavored prunes for more flavor, and then omit the lemon juice.

¼ cup mayonnaise or salad dressing

1 tablespoon chopped fresh or 1 teaspoon dried tarragon leaves

2 teaspoons lemon juice

2 cups cubed cooked chicken

1 cup chopped celery (about 2 medium stalks)

1 cup golden raisins

1 cup pitted prunes, cut in half

¼ cup chopped macadamia nuts or sliced almonds, toasted

Mix mayonnaise, tarragon and lemon juice in medium bowl. Add remaining ingredients; toss. *4 servings.*

NUTRITION INFORMATION PER SERVING

1 serving		Percent of U.S. RDA	
Calories	515	Vitamin A	10%
Protein, g	24	Vitamin C	4%
Carbohydrate, g	58	Calcium	6%
Fat, g	21	Iron	20%
Cholesterol, mg	65		
Sodium, mg	170		

Chicken Gazpacho Salad

Southwest Chicken Salad

If you are using regular French dressing, add ¼ teaspoon ground cumin to dressing to get a southwest flavor.

> *2 cups cubed cooked chicken*
>
> *1 cup chopped jicama*
>
> *½ cup chopped Anaheim chiles (about 2 medium) or green bell pepper (about 1 small)*
>
> *¼ cup Mexican or French dressing*
>
> *1 can (15 to 16 ounces) pinto beans, drained*
>
> *1 can (8 ounces) whole kernel corn, drained*
>
> *Lettuce leaves*

Mix all ingredients except lettuce. Serve on lettuce leaves. *4 servings.*

NUTRITION INFORMATION PER SERVING

1 serving		*Percent of U.S. RDA*	
Calories	360	Vitamin A	4%
Protein, g	29	Vitamin C	20%
Carbohydrate, g	34	Calcium	6%
Fat, g	12	Iron	20%
Cholesterol, mg	65		
Sodium, mg	580		

Chicken–Wild Rice Salad

> *1 cup uncooked wild rice*
>
> *2½ cups water*
>
> *2 cups cubed cooked chicken*
>
> *2 cups sliced mushrooms*
>
> *2 cups bite-size pieces spinach*
>
> *¼ cup chopped green onions (2 to 3 medium)*
>
> *Balsamic Dressing (below)*

Place wild rice in wire strainer. Run cold water through rice, lifting rice with fingers to clean thoroughly. Heat wild rice and water to boiling in 2-quart saucepan, stirring once; reduce heat. Cover and simmer 40 to 50 minutes or until wild rice is tender. Fluff wild rice with fork. Prepare Balsamic Dressing. Mix wild rice, chicken, mushrooms, spinach and green onions in large bowl. Pour dressing over salad; toss. *6 servings.*

BALSAMIC DRESSING

> *⅓ cup vegetable oil*
>
> *¼ cup balsamic or red wine vinegar*
>
> *1 teaspoon chopped fresh or ¼ teaspoon dried thyme leaves*
>
> *½ teaspoon salt*

Beat all ingredients, using wire whisk.

NUTRITION INFORMATION PER SERVING

1 serving		*Percent of U.S. RDA*	
Calories	310	Vitamin A	16%
Protein, g	19	Vitamin C	4%
Carbohydrate, g	25	Calcium	4%
Fat, g	15	Iron	12%
Cholesterol, mg	40		
Sodium, mg	230		

Turkey Fajita Pita

4 pita breads (6 inches in diameter)

¼ cup thick-and-chunky salsa

1 pound thinly sliced cooked deli turkey

1 small red bell pepper, cut into ¼-inch strips

¼ cup finely chopped red onion

4 slices (1 ounce each) Monterey Jack cheese

Cut each pita bread in half; separate to form pockets. Spoon salsa into pockets. Top with turkey, bell pepper, onion and cheese. *4 sandwiches.*

NUTRITION INFORMATION PER SERVING

1 sandwich		Percent of U.S. RDA	
Calories	520	Vitamin A	16%
Protein, g	49	Vitamin C	16%
Carbohydrate, g	50	Calcium	28%
Fat, g	14	Iron	20%
Cholesterol, mg	120		
Sodium, mg	820		

Grilled Stilton and Chicken Sandwiches

The whole family will enjoy this sandwich, though you may want to substitute Cheddar for children—or others—who may not like the strong-tasting Stilton cheese.

¼ cup mayonnaise or salad dressing

12 slices crusty sourdough bread, about ½ inch thick

6 slices (1 ounce each) Stilton or Cheddar cheese

1 pound thinly sliced cooked deli chicken

2 medium pears, peeled and sliced

¼ cup (½ stick) margarine or butter, softened

Spread mayonnaise on 6 slices bread. Top with cheese, chicken, pears and remaining bread. Spread 1 teaspoon margarine over each top slice of bread.

Place sandwiches, margarine sides down, in skillet. Spread remaining margarine over top slices of bread. Cook uncovered over low heat 15 to 20 minutes, turning once, until sandwiches are golden brown and cheese is melted. *6 sandwiches.*

TO GRILL: Grease hinged wire grill basket. Place sandwiches in basket. Cover and grill 5 to 6 inches from medium coals 15 to 20 minutes, turning once, until sandwiches are golden brown.

NUTRITION INFORMATION PER SERVING

1 sandwich		Percent of U.S. RDA	
Calories	540	Vitamin A	16%
Protein, g	35	Vitamin C	*
Carbohydrate, g	37	Calcium	20%
Fat, g	28	Iron	14%
Cholesterol, mg	95		
Sodium, mg	660		

Baked Turkey Sandwiches

⅓ cup margarine or butter, softened

1 tablespoon Dijon mustard

1 tablespoon instant minced onion

1 teaspoon poppy seed

8 kaiser rolls, split

1½ pounds thinly sliced smoked deli turkey

8 slices (1 ounce each) Swiss cheese

Heat oven to 350°. Mix margarine, mustard, onion and poppy seed. Spread margarine mixture over rolls. Fill rolls with turkey and cheese. Wrap each sandwich in aluminum foil. Bake 20 to 30 minutes or until sandwiches are hot and cheese is melted. *8 sandwiches.*

TO GRILL: Wrap each sandwich in aluminum foil. Cover and grill 5 to 6 inches from medium coals 15 to 20 minutes or until sandwiches are hot and cheese is melted.

NUTRITION INFORMATION PER SERVING

1 sandwich		*Percent of U.S. RDA*	
Calories	420	Vitamin A	14%
Protein, g	27	Vitamin C	*
Carbohydrate, g	33	Calcium	32%
Fat, g	20	Iron	12%
Cholesterol, mg	65		
Sodium, mg	1500		

Mediterranean Sandwich

A baguette is a traditional French bread that's long and thin and can be up to 2 feet long. Many supermarket bakery sections carry fresh baguettes. If they are unavailable, you can also use regular French bread.

2 cups cubed cooked chicken

½ cup chopped red bell pepper (about 1 small)

½ cup chopped cucumber

½ cup shredded mozzarella cheese (2 ounces)

¼ cup mayonnaise or salad dressing

2 teaspoons chopped fresh or ½ teaspoon dried oregano leaves

1 can (4¼ ounces) chopped ripe olives, drained

1 baguette (14 to 16 inches), cut horizontally in half

Set oven control to broil. Mix all ingredients except baguette. Spoon about 1½ cups chicken mixture onto each bread half. Place on ungreased cookie sheet. Broil with tops 4 to 6 inches from heat about 5 minutes or until hot. Cut each into 3 slices. *6 servings.*

NUTRITION INFORMATION PER SERVING

1 serving		*Percent of U.S. RDA*	
Calories	415	Vitamin A	8%
Protein, g	24	Vitamin C	10%
Carbohydrate, g	48	Calcium	16%
Fat, g	14	Iron	20%
Cholesterol, mg	50		
Sodium, mg	750		

Italian Sausage Sandwiches

This is a great recipe for a family barbecue or an easy get-together. Let everyone put on his or her own vegetables and spaghetti sauce, and create the perfect sandwich.

> *6 links turkey Italian sausage (about 1 pound)*
>
> *2 Anaheim chiles or 1 small green bell pepper, cut into ¼-inch slices*
>
> *1 small red bell pepper, cut into ¼-inch slices*
>
> *1 medium sweet onion (Bermuda, Maui, Spanish or Vidalia), sliced*
>
> *1 small fennel bulb, cut into ¼-inch slices*
>
> *6 hoagie buns, split*

Cook sausage links in 10-inch skillet over medium heat about 20 minutes, turning frequently, until sausage is no longer pink in center; drain. Stir in remaining ingredients except buns. Cook about 5 minutes, stirring occasionally, until onion is crisp-tender. Place sausages in buns. Top with onion mixture. Serve with spaghetti sauce if desired. *6 sandwiches.*

TO GRILL: Grill sausage links uncovered 4 to 5 inches from medium coals 20 to 25 minutes, turning frequently, until sausage is no longer pink in center. Place remaining ingredients except buns on aluminum foil; seal foil tightly. Grill uncovered 6 to 8 minutes, turning once, until onion is tender.

NUTRITION INFORMATION PER SERVING

1 sandwich		*Percent of U.S. RDA*	
Calories	405	Vitamin A	14%
Protein, g	23	Vitamin C	10%
Carbohydrate, g	49	Calcium	14%
Fat, g	13	Iron	16%
Cholesterol, mg	60		
Sodium, mg	1170		

Tex-Mex Chile Dogs

Black beans cooked with tomato sauce and chile powder make an easy version of chile dogs. Try cheese with jalapeños if your family likes spicy foods.

1 can (15 ounces) black beans, rinsed and drained

1 can (8 ounces) tomato sauce

1 to 2 teaspoons chile powder

6 turkey or chicken franks

6 frankfurter buns, split

½ cup shredded process cheese spread loaf with jalapeños or plain process cheese spread loaf (2 ounces)

2 slices (1 ounce each) cheddar cheese, cut into strips

Mix beans, tomato sauce and chile powder in 1-quart saucepan. Cook over medium-high heat about 6 minutes, stirring occasionally, until hot. Set oven control to broil. Place franks on rack in broiler pan. Broil with tops about 3 inches from heat 5 to 8 minutes, turning once, until brown. Place franks in buns. Top with bean mixture and cheese strips. *6 sandwiches.*

TO GRILL: Mix beans, tomato sauce and chile powder in square aluminum foil pan, 8×8×2 inches. Cover with aluminum foil. Cover and grill about 4 inches from medium coals 6 to 8 minutes or until hot. Cover and grill franks 5 to 8 minutes, turning once, until brown.

NUTRITION INFORMATION PER SERVING

1 sandwich		*Percent of U.S. RDA*	
Calories	355	Vitamin A	6%
Protein, g	17	Vitamin C	*
Carbohydrate, g	40	Calcium	20%
Fat, g	14	Iron	18%
Cholesterol, mg	60		
Sodium, mg	1140		

Tex-Mex Chile Dogs

Mix-and-Match Pasta Salads

Creative pasta salads can be as easy as one, two, three when you use precooked pasta and the wonderful range of ingredients in this easy-to-use chart. Add a splash of your favorite bottled salad dressing, and you'll have a pleasing meal in minutes!

DIRECTIONS:

Select ingredients from each category as indicated in the chart below; mix together in a large bowl and store covered in refrigerator. Each combination will make four servings.

MIX-AND-MATCH PASTA SALAD CHART

Chicken or Turkey
(choose 1)

- 1½ cups cubed, chopped or shredded cooked chicken or turkey

Pasta or Grains
(2 cups cooked—choose 1 or 2)

- Barley
- Bulgur
- Couscous
- Elbow, ring or shell macaroni
- Farfalle (bowties)
- Mostaccioli
- Orzo
- Quinoa
- Radditore
- Rice
- Rigatoni
- Rotini
- Tortellini
- Wagon Wheels
- Whole wheat berries
- Ziti

Vegetable and Fruit Additions
(choose 1 cup per serving)

- Avocado (cubed or sliced)
- Apple (chopped)
- Bell pepper (chopped)
- Berries (whole or sliced)
- Broccoli (chopped)
- Carrot (sliced or shredded)
- Celery (chopped)
- Cucumber (chopped or sliced)
- Fennel bulb (chopped or sliced)
- Canned fruit (drained)
- Green onion (chopped or sliced)
- Jicama (chopped or shredded)
- Kohlrabi (chopped or sliced)
- Pineapple (chopped)
- Pea pods
- Radishes (sliced)
- Sugar snap peas
- Sun-dried tomatoes packed in oil (chopped)
- Tomatoes or cherry tomatoes
- Yellow summer squash (chopped or sliced)
- Zucchini (chopped or sliced)

MIX-AND-MATCH PASTA SALAD CHART (*continued*)

Additional Ingredients

- Bacon
- Canned beans (drained)
- Cheese (diced or shredded)
- Fresh herbs (chopped)

- Hard-cooked eggs
- Nuts
- Olives (chopped, sliced or whole)

- Raisins
- Red pepper (cayenne) or red pepper sauce
- Salt and pepper to taste

Dressing
(choose 1 or 2 to equal 1 cup)

- Mayonnaise or salad dressing (regular or reduced-fat)
- Plain yogurt (regular or reduced-fat)

- Purchased salad dressing, any type

- Sour cream (regular or reduced-fat)

Easy Chicken Sub

¼ cup honey-Dijon dressing

1 loaf (8 ounces) French bread, cut horizontally in half

½ pound thinly sliced cooked deli chicken

¼ cup shredded carrot

½ cup thinly sliced jicama

4 slices (1 ounce each) Colby or Cheddar cheese

Spread dressing over bottom of bread loaf. Layer chicken, carrot, jicama and cheese evenly on bottom of loaf. Top with top of loaf. Cut into 4 slices. *4 servings.*

NUTRITION INFORMATION PER SERVING

1 serving		Percent of U.S. RDA	
Calories	465	Vitamin A	16%
Protein, g	30	Vitamin C	*
Carbohydrate, g	43	Calcium	22%
Fat, g	19	Iron	14%
Cholesterol, mg	75		
Sodium, mg	580		

Danish Open-face Sandwiches

If you like more variety, try spreading some of the sandwiches with butter, mayonnaise or mustard instead of pâté.

1 container (7 ounces) liver pâté

1 loaf (16 ounces) thinly sliced rye bread

¼ pound thinly sliced cooked deli chicken

¼ pound thinly sliced cooked deli turkey

¼ pound thinly sliced Havarti or Gouda cheese

2 hard-cooked eggs, sliced

1 can (4½ ounces) tiny shrimp, rinsed and drained

2 medium tomatoes, thinly sliced

Dill weed sprigs

Parsley sprigs

Spread pâté over bread slices. Layer remaining ingredients on pâté. Layer ingredients in a different order for each sandwich if desired. *16 open-face sandwiches.*

NUTRITION INFORMATION PER SERVING

1 sandwich		Percent of U.S. RDA	
Calories	145	Vitamin A	36%
Protein, g	12	Vitamin C	*
Carbohydrate, g	11	Calcium	6%
Fat, g	6	Iron	10%
Cholesterol, mg	105		
Sodium, mg	250		

Open-face Chicken Sandwiches

1½ cups cut-up cooked chicken or turkey

⅓ cup mayonnaise or salad dressing

¼ cup slivered almonds, toasted

¼ cup thinly sliced celery

1 tablespoon chopped green onion

1 medium tomato, thinly sliced

2 whole wheat English muffins, split and toasted

1 container (6 ounces) frozen avocado dip, thawed

Mix chicken, mayonnaise, almonds, celery and onion. Place tomato slices on each muffin half. Spoon chicken mixture onto tomatoes. Spoon avocado dip onto chicken mixture. *4 open-face sandwiches.*

NUTRITION INFORMATION PER SERVING

1 serving		*Percent of U.S. RDA*	
Calories	395	Vitamin A	10%
Protein, g	20	Vitamin C	12%
Carbohydrate, g	22	Calcium	6%
Fat, g	25	Iron	14%
Cholesterol, mg	55		
Sodium, mg	350		

Turkey Bean Pot

These old-fashioned baked beans are slightly sweet—if you like more savory flavor, reduce brown sugar to 2 tablespoons.

1 pound fresh turkey bratwurst

1 cup chopped onion (about 1 large)

1 cup ketchup

¼ cup packed brown sugar

1 tablespoon Worcestershire sauce

1 tablespoon Dijon mustard

1 can (15 to 16 ounces) great northern beans, drained

1 can (15 to 16 ounces) pinto beans, drained

1 can (15 ounces) black beans, rinsed and drained

Heat oven to 375°. Cook bratwurst and onion in 10-inch skillet over medium heat about 20 minutes, turning bratwurst and stirring onion occasionally, until bratwurst is no longer pink in center; drain. Cut bratwurst into 2-inch pieces. Mix bratwurst, onion and remaining ingredients in 2-quart casserole or bean pot. Cover and bake 40 to 45 minutes or until hot. *6 servings.*

NUTRITION INFORMATION PER SERVING

1 serving		*Percent of U.S. RDA*	
Calories	490	Vitamin A	4%
Protein, g	26	Vitamin C	6%
Carbohydrate, g	65	Calcium	22%
Fat, g	14	Iron	36%
Cholesterol, mg	80		
Sodium, mg	1760		

Curried Chicken Sandwich

1 cup diced cooked chicken or turkey

⅓ cup mayonnaise or salad dressing

¼ cup sliced celery

2 tablespoons chopped peanuts

1 tablespoon chutney

½ teaspoon curry powder

Lettuce

8 slices raisin bread, toasted if desired

Mix all ingredients except lettuce and bread. Place lettuce on 4 slices bread. Spoon about ⅓ cup chicken mixture on each. Top with remaining slices bread. *4 sandwiches.*

NUTRITION INFORMATION PER SERVING

1 serving		*Percent of U.S. RDA*	
Calories	365	Vitamin A	6%
Protein, g	15	Vitamin C	4%
Carbohydrate, g	31	Calcium	6%
Fat, g	20	Iron	14%
Cholesterol, mg	40		
Sodium, mg	350		

Chicken-Rice Casserole

¼ cup (½ stick) margarine or butter

⅓ cup all-purpose flour

½ teaspoon salt

⅛ teaspoon pepper

1 cup chicken broth

1½ cups milk

2 cups cut-up cooked chicken

1½ cups cooked white or wild rice

⅓ cup chopped green bell pepper

¼ cup slivered almonds

2 tablespoons diced pimiento

1 can (3 ounces) sliced mushrooms, drained

Chopped fresh parsley, if desired

Heat oven to 350°. Heat margarine in 1½-quart saucepan over low heat until melted. Stir in flour, salt and pepper. Cook, stirring constantly, until mixture is smooth and bubbly; remove from heat. Stir in broth and milk. Heat to boiling, stirring constantly. Boil and stir 1 minute. Stir in remaining ingredients except parsley.

Pour into ungreased 1½-quart casserole. Bake uncovered 40 to 45 minutes. Sprinkle with parsley. *6 to 8 servings.*

NUTRITION INFORMATION PER SERVING

1 serving		*Percent of U.S. RDA*	
Calories	315	Vitamin A	16%
Protein, g	20	Vitamin C	4%
Carbohydrate, g	25	Calcium	10%
Fat, g	15	Iron	12%
Cholesterol, mg	45		
Sodium, mg	700		

Chicken Tetrazzini

1 package (7 ounces) spaghetti, broken
into thirds
¼ cup (½ stick) margarine or butter
¼ cup all-purpose flour
½ teaspoon salt
¼ teaspoon pepper
1 cup chicken broth
1 cup whipping (heavy) cream
2 tablespoons sherry or water
2 cups cubed cooked chicken
1 can (3 ounces) sliced mushrooms,
drained
½ cup grated Parmesan cheese

Heat oven to 350°. Cook spaghetti as directed on package; drain. Heat margarine in large 2-quart saucepan over low heat until melted. Stir in flour, salt and pepper. Cook, stirring constantly, until mixture is smooth and bubbly; remove from heat. Stir in broth and cream. Heat to boiling, stirring constantly. Boil and stir 1 minute. Stir in sherry, spaghetti, chicken and mushrooms.

Pour into ungreased 2-quart casserole. Sprinkle with cheese. Bake uncovered about 30 minutes or until bubbly in center. *6 servings.*

NUTRITION INFORMATION PER SERVING

1 serving		*Percent of U.S. RDA*	
Calories	475	Vitamin A	24%
Protein, g	23	Vitamin C	*
Carbohydrate, g	33	Calcium	14%
Fat, g	28	Iron	14%
Cholesterol, mg	100		
Sodium, mg	620		

Mostaccioli with Italian Sausage

6 links turkey Italian sausage (about 1
pound)
1 package (16 ounces) mostaccioli (tube
shape) pasta
1 jar (14 ounces) spaghetti sauce
½ cup ricotta cheese
¼ cup grated Parmesan cheese

Cook sausage links in 10-inch skillet over medium heat about 20 minutes, turning frequently, until sausage is no longer pink in center; drain. Cut sausages into 2-inch pieces. Cook pasta as directed on package; drain. In same 10-inch skillet mix pasta, sausage pieces, spaghetti sauce and ricotta cheese; heat through. Sprinkle with Parmesan cheese. *6 servings.*

NUTRITION INFORMATION PER SERVING

1 serving		*Percent of U.S. RDA*	
Calories	600	Vitamin A	6%
Protein, g	28	Vitamin C	*
Carbohydrate, g	68	Calcium	14%
Fat, g	24	Iron	24%
Cholesterol, mg	60		
Sodium, mg	1400		

Pizza Mexicana

6 pita breads (6 inches in diameter)

1 can (15 ounces) tomato sauce with tomato bits

2 cups shredded or chopped cooked chicken

1 can (4 ounces) chopped green chiles, drained

1½ cups shredded taco-seasoned cheese (6 ounces)

Heat oven to 350°. Place pita breads on ungreased cookie sheet. Spread tomato sauce over pita breads. Top with chicken and chiles. Sprinkle with cheese. Bake 8 to 10 minutes or until pizzas are hot and cheese is melted. *6 servings.*

NUTRITION INFORMATION PER SERVING

1 pizza		Percent of U.S. RDA	
Calories	450	Vitamin A	14%
Protein, g	30	Vitamin C	10%
Carbohydrate, g	53	Calcium	22%
Fat, g	13	Iron	18%
Cholesterol, mg	70		
Sodium, mg	1220		

Hawaiian Pizza

1 Italian bread shell or prepared pizza crust (12 inches in diameter)

1 can (8 ounces) tomato sauce

2 cups cubed cooked chicken

1 can (8 ounces) pineapple tidbits, well drained

2 tablespoons sliced green onions

1 cup shredded mozzarella cheese (4 ounces)

Heat oven to 400°. Place bread shell on ungreased cookie sheet. Spread tomato sauce over bread shell. Top with chicken and pineapple. Sprinkle with onions and cheese. Bake 8 to 10 minutes or until pizza is hot and cheese is melted. *6 servings.*

NUTRITION INFORMATION PER SERVING

1 slice		Percent of U.S. RDA	
Calories	440	Vitamin A	6%
Protein, g	26	Vitamin C	4%
Carbohydrate, g	50	Calcium	16%
Fat, g	15	Iron	22%
Cholesterol, mg	50		
Sodium, mg	1080		

Hawaiian Pizza

CHAPTER

8

Condiments

A "little something" is always welcome with chicken and turkey, so we have collected an enticing array of condiments to choose from. While Pan Gravy is always classic, you may want to try new ideas such as Pear Cranberry Chutney and Curried Peach Sauce. You'll find wonderful ideas here that will spice your meals very nicely.

Try Pesto with grilled chicken, or Apricot-Rosemary Salsa spooned over poached chicken breasts. Honey-Mustard Spread will add zest to a sandwich, as would Dill Sandwich Spread. Use these condiments in any way you wish to create your own sensational meals!

Apricot-Rosemary Salsa (page 196), Pear Cranberry Chutney (page 197), Tropical Fruit Salsa (page 195)

Honey-Mustard Spread

½ cup mayonnaise or salad dressing

1 tablespoon honey

1 tablespoon Dijon mustard

Mix all ingredients until smooth. *About ⅔ cup spread.*

NUTRITION INFORMATION PER SERVING

1 tablespoon		*Percent of U.S. RDA*	
Calories	80	Vitamin A	*
Protein, g	0	Vitamin C	*
Carbohydrate, g	2	Calcium	*
Fat, g	8	Iron	*
Cholesterol, mg	10		
Sodium, mg	75		

Dill Sandwich Spread

Serve this tasty spread on a chicken sandwich or as a sauce on grilled chicken.

¼ cup mayonnaise or salad dressing

¼ cup soft cream cheese

2 tablespoons finely chopped peeled cucumber

1 tablespoon chopped fresh or 1 teaspoon dried dill weed

Mix all ingredients. *About ½ cup spread.*

NUTRITION INFORMATION PER SERVING

1 serving		*Percent of U.S. RDA*	
Calories	75	Vitamin A	*
Protein, g	0	Vitamin C	*
Carbohydrate, g	1	Calcium	*
Fat, g	8	Iron	*
Cholesterol, mg	10		
Sodium, mg	60		

Tropical Fruit Salsa

1 cup pineapple chunks

1 tablespoon finely chopped red onion

1 tablespoon chopped fresh cilantro

2 tablespoons lime juice

2 kiwifruit, peeled and chopped

1 mango, peeled, pitted and chopped

1 papaya, peeled, pitted and chopped

*1 jalapeño chile, seeded and finely
    chopped*

Mix all ingredients in glass or plastic bowl. Cover and refrigerate 1 to 2 hours. Serve at room temperature. *About 2 cups salsa.*

NUTRITION INFORMATION PER SERVING

¼ cup		Percent of U.S. RDA	
Calories	60	Vitamin A	16%
Protein, g	1	Vitamin C	50%
Carbohydrate, g	14	Calcium	2%
Fat, g	0	Iron	2%
Cholesterol, mg	0		
Sodium, mg	5		

Fresh Tomato Salsa

If you like a hot salsa, leave the seeds in the jalapeño chile.

2 cups chopped tomatoes (about 2 large)

*1 cup chopped seeded cucumber (about 1
    small)*

2 tablespoons sliced green onion

2 tablespoons balsamic vinegar

¼ teaspoon salt

*1 jalapeño chile, seeded and finely
    chopped*

Mix all ingredients in glass or plastic bowl. Cover and refrigerate 1 to 2 hours. Serve at room temperature. *About 2½ cups salsa.*

NUTRITION INFORMATION PER SERVING

¼ cup		Percent of U.S. RDA	
Calories	10	Vitamin A	6%
Protein, g	0	Vitamin C	12%
Carbohydrate, g	3	Calcium	*
Fat, g	0	Iron	2%
Cholesterol, mg	0		
Sodium, mg	60		

Apricot-Rosemary Salsa

For a flavorful and elegant entrée, serve this salsa with chicken poached in apricot nectar.

1 can (5½ ounces) apricot nectar

½ cup chopped dried apricots

1 tablespoon chopped shallots

¾ cup chopped roma (plum) tomatoes (about 3 medium)

2 teaspoons chopped fresh or ½ teaspoon crushed dried rosemary leaves

1 teaspoon lemon juice

⅛ teaspoon ground cinnamon

⅛ teaspoon ground ginger

2 tablespoons chopped fresh parsley

Mix apricot nectar, apricots and shallots in 2-quart saucepan. Heat to boiling over medium heat; reduce heat. Simmer, uncovered, 3 to 5 minutes or until most of nectar is absorbed. Stir in remaining ingredients except parsley; heat thoroughly. Stir in parsley. Serve over chicken. Serve warm or cold. *About 1 cup salsa.*

NUTRITION INFORMATION PER SERVING

¼ cup		Percent of U.S. RDA	
Calories	75	Vitamin A	20%
Protein, g	1	Vitamin C	6%
Carbohydrate, g	18	Calcium	2%
Fat, g	0	Iron	6%
Cholesterol, mg	0		
Sodium, mg	10		

Crunchy Vegetable Relish

2 cups finely shredded green cabbage

1 cup coarsely shredded carrots (about 2 medium)

1 cup chopped zucchini (about 1 medium)

½ cup sugar

¼ cup chopped red onion

¼ cup balsamic or cider vinegar

½ teaspoon ground mustard

1 can (11 ounces) whole kernel corn with red and green peppers, undrained

Mix all ingredients in glass or plastic bowl. Cover and refrigerate at least 8 hours or overnight. Use a slotted spoon to serve. *About 4 cups relish.*

NUTRITION INFORMATION PER SERVING

¼ cup		Percent of U.S. RDA	
Calories	50	Vitamin A	12%
Protein, g	1	Vitamin C	2%
Carbohydrate, g	12	Calcium	*
Fat, g	0	Iron	*
Cholesterol, mg	0		
Sodium, mg	50		

Four-Fruit Relish

1 cup fresh raspberries

1 cup chopped pineapple

⅓ cup mashed banana (about 1 small)

1 tablespoon sugar

1 small seedless orange, peeled and chopped

Mix all ingredients in glass or plastic bowl. Cover and refrigerate 2 to 3 hours. Serve at room temperature. *About 2 cups relish.*

NUTRITION INFORMATION PER SERVING

1 tablespoon		*Percent of U.S. RDA*	
Calories	40	Vitamin A	*
Protein, g	0	Vitamin C	10%
Carbohydrate, g	10	Calcium	*
Fat, g	0	Iron	*
Cholesterol, mg	0		
Sodium, mg	0		

Pear-Cranberry Chutney

3 cups coarsely chopped peeled pears (about 3 medium)

1 cup dried or fresh cranberries

¾ cup sugar

½ cup cider vinegar

2 teaspoons finely chopped gingerroot

½ teaspoon ground cinnamon

¼ teaspoon ground cloves

Mix all ingredients in 2-quart saucepan. Heat to boiling; reduce heat. Cook over low heat about 1 hour, stirring frequently, until thickened. Cool slightly. Cover and refrigerate up to 2 weeks. Serve at room temperature. *About 2½ cups chutney.*

NUTRITION INFORMATION PER SERVING

¼ cup		*Percent of U.S. RDA*	
Calories	100	Vitamin A	*
Protein, g	0	Vitamin C	2%
Carbohydrate, g	25	Calcium	*
Fat, g	0	Iron	2%
Cholesterol, mg	0		
Sodium, mg	5		

Spicy Barbecue Sauce

1 tablespoon margarine or butter

¼ cup finely chopped onion (about 1 small)

1 clove garlic, finely chopped

½ cup ketchup

1 tablespoon vinegar

1 teaspoon Worcestershire sauce

¼ teaspoon ground mustard

¼ teaspoon ground red pepper (cayenne)

Dash of pepper

Heat margarine in 1-quart saucepan over medium heat until melted. Cook onion and garlic in margarine, stirring occasionally, until onion is tender. Stir in remaining ingredients. Cook until thoroughly heated. Brush sauce on chicken during last 15 minutes of grilling or broiling. Heat any remaining sauce to boiling; boil 1 minute. Serve with chicken. *About ½ cup sauce.*

NUTRITION INFORMATION PER SERVING

2 tablespoons		*Percent of U.S. RDA*	
Calories	65	Vitamin A	6%
Protein, g	0	Vitamin C	2%
Carbohydrate, g	10	Calcium	*
Fat, g	3	Iron	2%
Cholesterol, mg	0		
Sodium, mg	400		

Tarragon Mornay Sauce

2 tablespoons butter*

2 teaspoons all-purpose flour

1 teaspoon chicken bouillon granules

2 teaspoons chopped fresh or ½ teaspoon dried tarragon leaves

⅛ teaspoon white pepper

1 cup evaporated milk or half-and-half

⅓ cup shredded Gruyère or Swiss cheese

Heat butter in 2-quart saucepan over medium heat. Stir in flour and bouillon granules. Cook, stirring constantly, until smooth and bubbly. Stir in tarragon and pepper. Gradually stir in milk. Cook, stirring constantly, until slightly thickened. Add cheese, stir until melted. Serve immediately. *About 1 cup sauce.*

* Butter provides the best results in this recipe, but margarine may be used.

NUTRITION INFORMATION PER SERVING

2 tablespoons		Percent of U.S. RDA	
Calories	90	Vitamin A	4%
Protein, g	3	Vitamin C	*
Carbohydrate, g	4	Calcium	12%
Fat, g	7	Iron	*
Cholesterol, mg	20		
Sodium, mg	220		

Creamy Herb-Mushroom Sauce

This velvety smooth sauce will surely become a favorite. Try varying it with your favorite herbs such as dill, rosemary or tarragon.

½ cup (1 stick) margarine or butter

1 tablespoon finely chopped shallots

1 cup thinly sliced mushrooms

1 tablespoon all-purpose flour

1 tablespoon chopped fresh or 1 teaspoon dried thyme leaves

1 tablespoon chopped fresh parsley or 1 teaspoon dried parsley flakes

½ cup half-and-half

1 tablespoon dry white wine, if desired

Heat margarine in 2-quart saucepan over medium heat until melted. Stir in shallots and mushrooms. Cook, stirring occasionally, until tender. Stir in flour, thyme and parsley. Cook, stirring constantly, until slightly thickened. Remove from heat, gradually stir in half-and-half and wine until smooth. Cook, stirring constantly, until thickened. Serve immediately. *About 1 cup sauce.*

NUTRITION INFORMATION PER SERVING

2 tablespoons		Percent of U.S. RDA	
Calories	130	Vitamin A	16%
Protein, g	1	Vitamin C	*
Carbohydrate, g	2	Calcium	2%
Fat, g	13	Iron	2%
Cholesterol, mg	5		
Sodium, mg	140		

Creamy Herb-Mushroom Sauce

Chunky Gingered Applesauce

4 cups coarsely chopped peeled cooking apples (about 4 medium)

½ cup water

¼ cup finely chopped crystallized ginger

1 tablespoon packed brown sugar

¼ teaspoon ground cinnamon

Mix all ingredients except cinnamon in 2-quart saucepan. Cover and heat to boiling; reduce heat. Simmer 10 to 15 minutes or until apples are tender, stirring occasionally. Drain off any excess liquid. Stir in cinnamon. Serve warm or cold. *About 2 cups sauce.*

NUTRITION INFORMATION PER SERVING

¼ cup		Percent of U.S. RDA	
Calories	40	Vitamin A	*
Protein, g	0	Vitamin C	*
Carbohydrate, g	10	Calcium	*
Fat, g	0	Iron	*
Cholesterol, mg	0		
Sodium, mg	0		

Lemon-Ginger Sauce

Try our at-home version of sweet-and-sour sauce. It's great served over chicken or as a dipping sauce.

½ cup packed brown sugar

1 tablespoon cornstarch

¼ teaspoon ground ginger

⅓ cup lemon juice

½ cup water

Mix brown sugar, cornstarch and ginger in 2-quart saucepan. Stir in lemon juice and water. Cook over medium heat, stirring frequently, until clear and thickened. Serve warm. *About 1 cup sauce.*

NUTRITION INFORMATION PER SERVING

2 tablespoons		Percent of U.S. RDA	
Calories	60	Vitamin A	*
Protein, g	0	Vitamin C	*
Carbohydrate, g	15	Calcium	*
Fat, g	0	Iron	2%
Cholesterol, mg	0		
Sodium, mg	10		

Curried Peach Sauce

1 can (16 ounces) sliced peaches in juice, drained, reserving juice

2 tablespoons honey

1 tablespoon cornstarch

1 teaspoon curry powder

⅓ cup golden raisins

Chop peaches. Add enough water to reserved juice to make 1 cup. Mix juice mixture and honey in 2-quart saucepan. Stir in cornstarch and curry powder. Cook over medium heat, stirring frequently, until clear and thickened. Stir in peaches and raisins. Cook until thoroughly heated. Serve warm or cold. *About 2 cups sauce.*

NUTRITION INFORMATION PER SERVING

¼ cup		Percent of U.S. RDA	
Calories	55	Vitamin A	2%
Protein, g	0	Vitamin C	*
Carbohydrate, g	14	Calcium	*
Fat, g	0	Iron	2%
Cholesterol, mg	0		
Sodium, mg	5		

Pesto

Serve this delicious sauce with grilled chicken or add to pasta salads or hot cooked pasta.

1 cup firmly packed fresh basil leaves

6 tablespoons grated Parmesan or Romano cheese

6 tablespoons olive or vegetable oil

1 tablespoon pine nuts

2 cloves garlic

Place all ingredients in blender or food processor. Cover and blend on medium speed, or process, about 3 minutes, stopping occasionally to scrape sides, until smooth. Store covered in refrigerator. *About ½ cup sauce.*

NUTRITION INFORMATION PER SERVING

1 tablespoon		Percent of U.S. RDA	
Calories	130	Vitamin A	24%
Protein, g	3	Vitamin C	20%
Carbohydrate, g	3	Calcium	12%
Fat, g	12	Iron	16%
Cholesterol, mg	5		
Sodium, mg	95		

Pan Gravy

2 tablespoons poultry drippings (fat and juices)

2 tablespoons all-purpose flour

1 cup liquid (poultry juices, broth, water)*

¼ teaspoon salt

¼ teaspoon pepper

Place chicken or turkey on warm platter; keep warm while preparing gravy. Pour drippings from pan into bowl, leaving brown particles in pan. Return 2 tablespoons drippings to pan. (Measure accurately because too little fat makes gravy lumpy.)

Stir in flour. (Measure accurately so gravy is not greasy.) Cook over medium heat, stirring constantly, until mixture is smooth and bubbly; remove from heat. Stir in liquid. Heat to boiling, stirring constantly. Boil and stir 1 minute. Stir in a few drops browning sauce if desired. Stir in salt and pepper. *About 1 cup gravy.*

CREAMY GRAVY: Substitute milk or half-and-half for half of the liquid.

GIBLET GRAVY: Cook gizzard, heart and neck of poultry in 4 cups salted water 1 to 2 hours or until tender. Add liver the last 30 minutes. Remove meat from neck and finely chop with giblets. Substitute broth from giblets for the liquid. Stir giblets into gravy. Heat until hot.

THIN GRAVY: Decrease drippings to 1 tablespoon and flour to 1 tablespoon.

* Vegetable cooking water, tomato juice or vegetable juice can be used as part of liquid.

NUTRITION INFORMATION PER SERVING

2 tablespoons		Percent of U.S. RDA	
Calories	30	Vitamin A	2%
Protein, g	1	Vitamin C	*
Carbohydrate, g	2	Calcium	*
Fat, g	2	Iron	*
Cholesterol, mg	0		
Sodium, mg	190		

METRIC CONVERSION GUIDE

U.S. UNITS	CANADIAN METRIC	AUSTRALIAN METRIC
Volume		
1/4 teaspoon	1 mL	1 ml
1/2 teaspoon	2 mL	2 ml
1 teaspoon	5 mL	5 ml
1 tablespoon	15 mL	20 ml
1/4 cup	50 mL	60 ml
1/3 cup	75 mL	80 ml
1/2 cup	125 mL	125 ml
2/3 cup	150 mL	170 ml
3/4 cup	175 mL	190 ml
1 cup	250 mL	250 ml
1 quart	1 liter	1 liter
1 1/2 quarts	1.5 liter	1.5 liter
2 quarts	2 liters	2 liters
2 1/2 quarts	2.5 liters	2.5 liters
3 quarts	3 liters	3 liters
4 quarts	4 liters	4 liters
Weight		
1 ounce	30 grams	30 grams
2 ounces	55 grams	60 grams
3 ounces	85 grams	90 grams
4 ounces (1/4 pound)	115 grams	125 grams
8 ounces (1/2 pound)	225 grams	225 grams
16 ounces (1 pound)	455 grams	500 grams
1 pound	455 grams	1/2 kilogram

Measurements

Inches	Centimeters
1	2.5
2	5.0
3	7.5
4	10.0
5	12.5
6	15.0
7	17.5
8	20.5
9	23.0
10	25.5
11	28.0
12	30.5
13	33.0
14	35.5
15	38.0

Temperatures

Fahrenheit	Celsius
32°	0°
212°	100°
250°	120°
275°	140°
300°	150°
325°	160°
350°	180°
375°	190°
400°	200°
425°	220°
450°	230°
475°	240°
500°	260°

NOTE
The recipes in this cookbook have not been developed or tested using metric measures. When converting recipes to metric, some variations in quality may be noted.

Index

CREDITS

Betty Crocker Food and Publications Center
   Director: Marcia Copeland
   Editor: Lori Fox
   Recipe Development: Cathy Swanson and Julie
Turnbull
   Food Stylists: Cindy Lund and Katie McElroy
Nutrition Department
   Nutritionist: Elyse Cohen & Nancy Holmes
Photographic Services
   Photographer: Nanci Doonan Dixon